Coworkers And Other Clowns

Trapped With Idiots? This Is Your Escape Guide

Michelle Ward

Coworkers and Other Clowns
Part of *The Cheap Therapy Series*

Copyright © 2025 by Michelle Ward

All rights reserved. No part of this book may be reproduced, distributed, or transmitted in any form or by any means, including photocopying, recording, or other electronic or mechanical methods, without the prior written permission of the publisher, except in the case of brief quotations embodied in critical reviews and certain other noncommercial uses permitted by copyright law.

This book is a work of humor and satire. The characters, incidents, and dialogue are drawn from exaggerations, archetypes, and comedic observation. Any resemblance to actual persons, living or dead, employed or recently fired, is entirely coincidental (though if you think you recognize someone... you probably do).

For cheap therapy, office survival, and the occasional laugh.

Contents

Introduction: Welcome to the Circus	1
1. The Idea Thief	7
2. The Close Talker	19
3. Meet Calamity Jane	30
4. The Weird Smell Guy	40
5. The Career Olympian	53
6. Meet Pill-Popping Penny	66
7. The Inappropriate Dresser	76
8. The Meeting Hog	89
9. Half-Day Stella	100
10. Pass-the-Buck Pete	110
11. Transient Supermodel	121
12. The Retired-in-Spirit Guy	133

13. Over-Promoted Mystery Manager	144
14. Conclusion: Welcome to the Circus	154
Also by	157

Introduction: Welcome to the Circus

Why You Bought This Book

Let me guess you didn't stumble across this book by accident. You bought it because you've been there — trapped in a fluorescent-lit office where time slows down, sanity leaks away, and coworkers transform into caricatures of human dysfunction.

Maybe you were stuck in a meeting where someone said, *"Let's circle back"* so many times you started to wonder if you'd accidentally joined a cult. Maybe you had a boss corner you at the copier and unload his entire midlife crisis while you prayed for the toner to run out so you'd have an excuse to escape. Or maybe you simply stood at the water cooler, stared at the lukewarm "hydration station," and wished with every fiber of your soul that it dispensed vodka instead.

This book is for that moment. It's for every time you've thought: *Surely, it's not just me. Surely other people also work with lunatics.* Spoiler alert: you're not alone. The clowns are everywhere.

The Problem With Workplaces

Here's the dirty little secret nobody tells you in career workshops: the modern office is less about productivity and more about containment. It's a social experiment gone wrong, a mismatched collection of personalities forced into a windowless box with a dodgy coffee machine. The actual work? That's secondary. The real challenge is surviving the people you work with.

Because let's be honest: your job description never mentioned The Idea Thief who will parrot your every suggestion five minutes later like it was their own. It never warned you about The Close Talker, who confuses your personal space with a timeshare. And it definitely didn't cover how to cope with Half-Day Stella, the boss who crams an entire week's worth of criticism into three hours before vanishing until tomorrow.

And then there's HR. Oh, HR. In theory, the guardians of workplace harmony. In practice? The professional equivalent of a "thoughts and prayers" tweet. They'll host seminars on "Effective Communication in the Workplace" while ignoring the fact that The Weird Smell Guy has turned his cubicle into a biohazard. They'll rewrite the dress code three times a year but never answer the question of how The Transient Supermodel managed to expense a three-hour "working lunch" with a cardiologist.

We were promised collaboration, synergy, and "a positive team culture." What we got instead was a full-time seat at the human circus.

Why Laughter Is the Only Survival Strategy

At this point, you might be thinking: *But what if I try to change things?* Go ahead. Start a petition. Write an anonymous HR complaint. Suggest a new process to "streamline workflows." See how far that gets you.

The truth? Offices aren't designed to change. They're designed to absorb dysfunction like a sponge absorbs coffee stains. You can cry, you can rage-eat vending machine chips at 10:45 a.m., you can even polish up your LinkedIn profile while pretending to work. But laughter? That's the only survival tool that doesn't end in burnout or a disciplinary meeting.

Laughing at the chaos doesn't mean you're not frustrated. It means you've finally found the only coping mechanism that makes sense. This book isn't going to fix your office — if it could, I'd be billing corporate clients at $500 an hour. What it *will* do is help you spot the clowns, recognize their classic moves, and laugh hard enough to keep you from rage-quitting before payday.

The Cast of Clowns

This book is a field guide — a survival manual dressed up as comedy. Inside, you'll meet the archetypes you already know, but never had the chance to roast properly:

The Idea Thief — swooping in like a seagull on hot chips, stealing credit for things you said five minutes earlier.

The Close Talker — leaning so far into your personal space you're legally engaged by lunchtime.

Calamity Jane — permanently late, permanently hungover, and always one tequila away from mechanical bull-related workplace injuries.

Pill-Popping Penny — whose legs gave way before your standards did.

The Inappropriate Dressers — treating boardrooms like Vegas runways and presentations like peep shows.

The Transient Supermodel — using Big Pharma as her personal dating app, fishing for doctors instead of KPIs.

The Weird Smell Guy — commuting via dumpster and bringing it with him.

The Meeting Hog — speaking for forty-five minutes without once saying anything useful.

The Career Olympian — sprinting over colleagues in the race for promotion.

Half-Day Stella — clocking off at noon, but not before tearing you down.

Pass-the-Buck Pete — surviving forty years in banking by mastering the ancient art of email forwarding.

The Retired-in-Spirit Guy — two years from retirement but already clocked out.

The Over-Promoted Mystery Manager — clueless, useless, and indestructible.

Each one comes with a roast, their "classic moves," survival strategies, and a little Cheap Therapy activity to help you laugh while plotting your escape.

Rules of the Circus (A.K.A. The Cheap Therapy Commandments)

Before we begin, a few simple rules for navigating the workplace zoo:

Thou shalt not take clowns seriously. They thrive on your outrage. Laugh instead.

Thou shalt document everything. Not for justice — just for the comedy gold later.

Thou shalt master the art of fake enthusiasm. Sometimes nodding is the only way out.

Thou shalt keep snacks in your drawer. They solve 80% of workplace crises.

Thou shalt know when to mute your mic. Especially during Zoom & Gloom.

Thou shalt avoid eye contact during presentations. You never know what's about to fall out.

Thou shalt remember: HR won't save you. They're too busy writing memos about "team spirit."

Thou shalt laugh louder than you cry. If you can't laugh, you're doomed.

The Promise

By the end of this book, you'll either:

Feel a strange sense of relief that your office isn't the only circus in town, or

Finally admit that you're surrounded by clowns and the only sane response is to laugh.

You'll have coping strategies (snarky, not serious), bingo cards for survival, and the satisfaction of knowing that somewhere out there, someone else is also trapped in a two-hour meeting where the only decision made was to "revisit this next week."

So grab your coffee, your coping mechanisms, and maybe a flask disguised as a water bottle. Welcome to **Coworkers and Other Clowns**. The circus is in town — and unfortunately, you're on the payroll.

Chapter One
The Idea Thief

Welcome to the Theft Factory

You've seen them. Hell, you probably work within three swivel chairs of one. The Idea Thief. The most frustrating, infuriating, soul-sucking creature in the workplace food chain.

This clown doesn't contribute, doesn't innovate, and certainly doesn't create. What they do is lurk — like a seagull circling a picnic, waiting for you to look away so they can snatch your sandwich. You'll pour your heart into brainstorming, offer up a clever solution, and before the echo of your voice has even died in the conference room, they're swooping in with:

"**Yes, that's exactly what I was about to say.**"

No, Greg. It isn't. You weren't about to say anything. The only thing you were about to do was check your phone under the table to see if your Uber Eats order had arrived. You couldn't "about to say" your way out of a paper bag, let alone come up with something resembling an actual idea.

The Idea Thief isn't just lazy. They're a parasite with a lanyard. They sit in meetings with that fake "deep in thought" face, chin propped on one hand, pen hovering above a notebook like they're writing the next great novel. What are they really doing? Nothing. They're not strategizing. They're scanning the room like a vulture, waiting for a spark of originality to pounce on. And the worst part? Half the time, the boss believes them.

The Meeting Where Hope Goes to Die

Picture this: it's Monday morning. You've been caffeinated since 8 a.m. and have been mentally preparing for this strategy session all weekend. You've crafted a pitch. You've even practiced it in the shower. This is your moment.

You speak up, lay out your idea, and wait for the room to absorb the genius. Silence. A couple of nods. A cough. Maybe someone scribbles something on a Post-it. You think: Okay, they're just processing.

Fast-forward five minutes. The Idea Thief clears their throat, leans forward, and says, "You know, what we really need here is a customer loyalty program that rewards repeat business."

Exactly what you said. Word. For. Word.

Suddenly, the room lights up like they've just discovered fire. The boss beams, "Yes! That's brilliant! Why didn't we think of that sooner?" Heads nod so violently you worry about neck braces. Someone even whispers, "That could change everything."

Meanwhile, you're sitting there blinking, trying to keep your soul from leaving your body. Because you know — you absolutely know — you just said that. And nobody cared until Greg, the office seagull, repeated it with jazz hands.

If life were fair, this is the part where a spotlight would swing down, a booming voice would announce, "OBJECTION! STOLEN CONTENT!" and confetti would fall in your honor. Instead, you just sit there while Greg basks like he's won *Shark Tank*.

This is why meetings are hell. Not because of PowerPoint. Not because of length. But because of the intellectual shoplifters who make you question your very existence.

Why They're the Worst

The Idea Thief isn't just annoying. They're corrosive. They kill enthusiasm. They strangle creativity. They make you second-guess whether you should even bother opening your mouth again.

Because what's the point? Why do the work, take the risk, and pitch something original when you know Greg or Susan or Carl will just swoop in, repackage it, and strut away with the credit?

And here's the kicker: they *genuinely* think they're smart. They call it "adding value" or "shaping the conversation." But you and I both know it's theft. Not slick Ocean's Eleven theft. Not suave, tuxedo-clad theft. No — this is alleyway-pigeon theft. Discount-bin, knockoff-headphones theft. Karaoke-night-at-the-bar theft.

And somehow, they're proud of it.

Office Life as a Crime Scene

If you've ever wanted to see gaslighting in action, work with an Idea Thief. They're like workplace pickpockets. By the end of the meeting, you're not even sure you came up with the idea at all.

You'll start checking your notes mid-discussion, reassuring yourself you didn't hallucinate.

You'll walk out dazed, muttering, "I swear that was mine."

You'll lie awake at night replaying the meeting like some corporate Law & Order rerun, desperately trying to prove you were the original source.

In your mind, you're starring in *CSI: Conference Room*. Fluorescent lights hum overhead. A whiteboard marker lies in an evidence bag. Post-its are dusted for fingerprints. The detective leans over your notes and says, "Looks like the suspect repeated this idea... with intent."

Meanwhile, Greg is probably at the pub bragging about how he "led the discussion" and "really drove innovation today."

The Truth About Idea Thieves

Here's the reality: they don't steal because they're criminal masterminds. They steal because they're empty. If you tapped their forehead, it would echo. If you opened their brain, it would look like a storage unit rented by moths.

They're the kid who copied your homework and still managed to get a better grade because the teacher liked their haircut. Now they're adults in ill-fitting blazers, sucking the oxygen out of meetings while you quietly fantasize about pulling the fire alarm just to shut them up.

And Yet... They Prosper

The worst part is that they often get rewarded. Managers fall for it because The Idea Thief is loud, confident, and utterly shameless. They look the boss in the eye, deliver your idea with faux gravitas, and somehow it's "game-changing."

They're not innovators. They're cover bands. Corporate lip-sync artists. Bootleg-DVD salesmen. They're Britney Spears at a county fair lip-syncing "Toxic" — hitting the moves, mouthing the words, but producing nothing real. And yet people still clap.

Classic Moves of the Corporate Magpie

Wondering if you're working with one? Spot the signs:

The Parrot: You share a suggestion. Two minutes later, they repeat it slower, louder, with a hand flourish — and everyone claps like they've solved global warming.

The Buzzword Bandit: They add one meaningless phrase to disguise the theft.
You: "We should target customers with a loyalty program."
Them: "Yes! What if we implemented a *scalable* loyalty program that really *leverages synergy*?"
Boss: "Brilliant, Carl."

The Email Hijacker: The first to send the "Recap & Next Steps" email, drafted so it looks like they masterminded the whole thing. You're still stirring sugar into your coffee when their "official summary" lands.

The Elevator Pitch Sniper: Magically ends up in the elevator with management. By the time the doors open, *your* idea is *their* pilot project.

The Meeting Martyr: When praised, they sigh and say, "It was a team effort," as if that cancels out the theft. Spoiler: it makes it worse.

Every workplace has one of these characters. Some offices run entire bingo cards with them.

Why They Do It

Idea Thieves aren't creative. They're opportunists. Like pigeons in a park, they don't bake bread — they swoop in and steal it from your hand.

They crave recognition but avoid effort. They're addicted to applause but allergic to originality. Deep down, they know they'll never come up with anything real. So like a flea-market stall, they trade in imitation goods and pray nobody inspects too closely.

The Toll on Your Sanity

Working with an Idea Thief feels like living in a parallel universe where you're invisible. You'll explain a brilliant idea, get silence, then five minutes later it's applauded when stolen.

At first, you keep your cool. But inside, your brain is screaming: "Are you kidding me? I literally just said that. I was RIGHT HERE. Am I a ghost? Did I die in 2009 and nobody told me?"

So you adapt. You start timestamping emails at 3 a.m. just to prove ownership. You rehearse ideas like a stand-up set, complete with punchline timing, so nobody can miss it's yours. You fantasize about hiring a court stenographer for every meeting, or skywriting your pitch above the office before Greg can repeat it.

By week twelve, you're ready to tattoo your ideas on your forehead and walk into meetings shirtless just to be recognized. By week twenty? You're googling "portable polygraph test" and considering bringing it to Monday's team huddle.

Your therapist starts hearing sentences like, "What if Greg is secretly bugging my desk?" You daydream about employing a courtroom sketch artist to capture the moment you speak, timestamp included, just so history will know.

This is the psychological tax of working with an Idea Thief. They don't just steal your ideas. They steal your will to participate.

How to Survive the Thief

You can't fix them. You can only outplay them:

Paper Trail Everything: Send ideas before the meeting. That way, when Carl parrots you, you've already planted the flag.

Call Them Out — Politely Savage: When they repeat you, smile and say, "I'm glad you agree with what I just said." Say it enough times and watch them sweat.

Deploy Decoys: Drop a deliberately bad idea. Let them steal it. Then enjoy the fireworks. Workplace karma, served piping hot.

Out-Volume Them: If they shout, shout louder. Yes, the meeting may devolve into a gladiator arena, but at least you won't be invisible.

Rebrand Yourself: Accept your role as the genius behind the curtain. Ghostwriters, meme creators, unsung inventors — your work powers the show. One day, when Carl has to deliver solo, he'll collapse like a soufflé.

Bonus Toolkit: Anti-Theft Edition

Noise-cancelling headphones (to block their smug "yes, that's what I was going to say").
  A pre-meeting email cannon.
  A "bad idea notebook" filled with decoys.
  Duct tape (not for you).
  Real-Life Sightings
  The colleague who pitched your entire presentation as their "vision" — down to the jokes.
  The manager who stayed silent all quarter, then repeated your proposal to the exec team like they discovered electricity.
  The intern who "suddenly had a great idea" that sounded suspiciously like the one you'd explained to them over coffee yesterday.
  Each one is proof: Idea Thieves survive by feasting on decent people's work.

Bonus Activity: Idea Theft Bingo

Print this out, keep it in your notebook, and tick boxes as you play. First to five wins the imaginary right to leave early.
  Repeats your suggestion word-for-word.
Waits until the boss walks in before suddenly "having" the idea.
Adds "synergy" to disguise the theft.
Sends a smug summary email.
Gets praised while you choke on rage.

Says, "That's exactly what I was about to say."

"Accidentally" forgets to CC you.

Brags in the lunchroom.

Bingo! Your genius is fueling someone else's promotion.

Why Justice Never Comes

Here's the bitter pill: Idea Thieves don't just survive in corporate life — they thrive.

Not because they're competent. Not because they're visionary. But because the system accidentally rewards their worst traits. Bosses are too busy to track originality. They don't care who said it first; they care who said it loud enough to jot down before the next Zoom call.

A fictional study I'd like to believe is real found that 83% of managers couldn't remember who originated an idea ten minutes after the meeting ended. Another 12% thought the PowerPoint slide itself had come up with it. The final 5% admitted they were just hungry.

The Idea Thief knows this. They weaponize shamelessness. Meanwhile, you're in the trenches, running the spreadsheets, smoothing workflows, fixing disasters. You don't have time to shout from rooftops. You just want the damn project to work. And that's when they swoop in, packaging your brilliance like a dodgy Amazon reseller.

They get promoted. Again and again. You watch them scale the corporate ladder like contestants on Ninja Warrior — except instead of muscles and grit, their only skill is brazen plagiarism.

But here's the good news: eventually, they hit a ceiling. They get promoted so high they no longer have peers to steal from. Suddenly, they're expected to lead. To innovate. To *actually* think. And that's when it collapses. Their "vision" is a blurry photocopy. Their "strategy" is a Buzzword Bingo card set on shuffle. Their "innovation" is so laughably vague it could have come from a Magic 8-Ball.

Watching that crash? That's your prize. It won't erase the frustration, but there's something delicious about seeing an Idea Thief finally run out of brains to borrow.

Final Roast

So next time The Idea Thief parrots your brilliance, don't despair. Remember: you're the brain, they're the megaphone. You're the chef, they're the diner photographing the dish and pretending they cooked it.

They're the knockoff handbag at the corporate fashion show. From afar, they look impressive. Up close, you can see the seams splitting. They're the karaoke singer belting Whitney Houston — sure, they know the lyrics, but the voice isn't theirs.

The Idea Thief thinks they're building a reputation. What they're really building is a filing cabinet of empty credit. And when asked to open it, all that spills out is dust and buzzwords.

Here's the truth: you don't need their validation. Everyone with half a brain knows what's happening. They've seen you pitch. They've seen the thief parrot. They may not say it out loud, but they're laughing with you.

Fast-forward twenty years: Greg's retirement speech. He thanks his colleagues, his mentors, and accidentally plagiarizes the catering menu. Everyone claps politely while you — now thriving elsewhere — sip champagne and grin.

Because clowns can juggle, sure. But they can't invent fire.

So stop letting it eat at you. Stop begging HR to care. Instead, laugh. Laugh because you're the one with the ideas. Laugh because they'll never be more than a cover band. Laugh because one day, you'll move on to something better — and they'll still be stuck in the circus, juggling buzzwords for an audience that stopped clapping years ago.

And you? You'll be too busy doing the thing The Idea Thief never could: creating.

Chapter Two
The Close Talker

When Personal Space Isn't Personal

Some coworkers test your patience. Some test your tolerance. And then there's the Close Talker — the coworker who tests the very boundaries of physics.

This is the person who treats your personal bubble like communal property. They lean in like you're trading nuclear codes, even when the conversation is about printer ink. Their breath fogs your glasses, their tie brushes your shoulder, and you can identify their lunch by smell alone before they've finished describing it.

It doesn't matter where you are — at your desk, in the hallway, in the elevator, even in the bathroom — the Close Talker always manages to position themselves six inches from your nose, like you're starring in a low-budget soap opera together.

They don't just invade your space. They annex it. They colonize it. They roll out the flag, plant it firmly in your comfort zone, and declare, "This is now my territory."

And the worst part? They don't even notice. To them, you're not recoiling — you're engaged. You're not squirming — you're connected. In their minds, this is bonding. In reality, it's harassment by proximity.

The Monday Morning Encounter

Picture this: You've just sat down with your coffee, bracing for inbox Armageddon. You're two sips into pretending you're a functioning adult when suddenly, here comes Brian from Accounts, hovering at your desk like a vampire waiting for an invitation.

"So... how was your weekend?"

You lean back. He leans forward. You scoot an inch. He scoots closer. Before long, you're locked in an awkward office waltz, rolling halfway to the fire exit just to reclaim oxygen that hasn't been pre-breathed by Brian.

And Brian never gets the hint. He's standing so close you can smell the exact brand of his laundry detergent. His eyes flick across your desk like he's memorizing state secrets. He laughs too loudly at his own jokes, sending a warm coffee-scented breeze into your face.

The rest of the office pretends not to notice, but you see them. They're smirking out of the corners of their eyes, grateful it isn't them. Someone even swivels in their chair to watch the spectacle, because nothing brightens a Monday like secondhand suffocation.

By the time Brian leaves, you're gripping your mug like a flotation device, three feet from your desk, already googling "How early can you fake food poisoning and go home?"

The Copy Room Ambush

Another classic. You're minding your business, waiting for the copier to spit out your quarterly report. The calm hum of the machine, the gentle flicker of fluorescent lights — a rare pocket of peace.

Then you feel it: hot breath on your neck.

You turn, and there they are — standing so close you could pass for conjoined twins. Their chin nearly brushes your shoulder as they whisper, "Crazy about that toner shortage, huh?"

No, Sharon. Not crazy. What's crazy is that I can count your eyelashes while you monologue about printer supplies. What's crazy is that I can identify your cologne as "Department Store Tester No. 5." What's crazy is that I'm considering slamming my head inside the copier lid just to escape.

The Copy Room is their favorite hunting ground because you're trapped. You can't leave mid-print. Your report is spitting out page by agonizing page, and Sharon has you pinned like you're in a hostage negotiation.

By the time your report finishes, you're dizzy, sweating, and seriously considering printing an extra copy just to stall for a noise shield.

The Elevator Trauma

That sacred 30-second elevator silence? Gone.

The doors close. You exhale. Peace. Then boom — they pivot toward you, nose grazing yours, whispering about last night's reality show like you're under NDA.

You inch away. They inch closer. You press into the corner. They lean diagonally across the button panel like a fog machine in khakis.

By floor six, you've stopped listening. By floor eight, you're praying for a mechanical failure. By floor ten, you've accepted death.

And when the doors open, they step out smiling, convinced you've just shared intimacy. Meanwhile, you're pricing stair-climbing shoes because you'll never set foot in an elevator again.

The Breakroom Siege

You've microwaved leftovers. You just want two minutes of peace while your sad pasta rotates. Enter the Close Talker.

They plant themselves in front of the microwave door, leaning in like they're analyzing your Tupperware for clues. "Mmm, smells good — what's that?"

It doesn't matter what you answer. You could say "nuclear waste" and they'd still inch closer to inhale. Suddenly you're defending your ravioli like a raccoon guarding trash.

And when the microwave dings? They don't move. They stand there, narrating their fantasy football league while your food sits hostage behind the glass.

The Bathroom Horror

There are few sacred spaces left in office life. The bathroom should be one. But not to a Close Talker.

You're at the sink, washing your hands, eyes glued to the mirror to avoid small talk. And then — there they are, leaning in, chatting about Q3 revenue like it's the perfect time. Their reflection is right beside yours, two inches away, like you've been cast in a buddy-cop show you never auditioned for.

They dry their hands on the paper towels directly next to yours. They follow you to the door. They exit at the exact same time, step for step, turning your walk back to the desk into a side-by-side parade of discomfort.

The Parking Lot Pursuit

You think you're free. You've clocked out, bag slung over your shoulder, car keys in hand. The fresh air hits. And then — footsteps.

"Hey, wait up!"

They appear at your side, instantly syncing their pace with yours, half a step too close, narrating their commute in excruciating detail. You edge toward your car. They edge with you. You unlock the door. They lean against the frame like they're about to carjack you with small talk.

By the time you escape, you've inhaled so much of their aftershave you can taste it.

The Conference Call Creep

Even remote work doesn't save you. On Zoom, they lean into the camera until you can count their pores. It's as though they're trying to climb through the screen.

They angle themselves so close to their webcam you get a panoramic view of their nasal cavity. They laugh directly into their microphone, sending digital hot breath straight through your headset. They say, "Don't you feel like this is more personal than email?"

No, Kevin. This isn't personal. This is paranormal.

Classic Moves of the Close Talker

The Whisper Shout: Inches from your face, volume set to stadium-rock.

The Desk Leaner: One hand on your desk, the other on your mouse. Congratulations, you're kidnapped.

The Coffee Breather: Post-espresso halitosis strong enough to kill a cactus.

The Meeting Hoverer: Refuses a chair, looms directly behind you, murmuring like an unwanted motivational speaker.

The Surprise Toucher: Back pats, arm squeezes, or worse — the handshake that never ends.

Office Life with a Close Talker

The Close Talker rewires your brain. You stop listening to words because your inner monologue is just: "Back. Up. Back. Up. BACK. UP."

You start plotting escape routes from your own cubicle. You sprint to the bathroom like it's an Olympic event. You fantasize about installing a moat or requesting a restraining order that specifies a five-foot radius.

Over time, you develop a sixth sense. You can feel them coming. A disturbance in the air pressure. A ripple in the office force.

Suddenly you're ducking into the supply closet to avoid another unsolicited story about their cat's digestive problems.

Why They're the Worst

Because unlike the Idea Thief, the Close Talker isn't stealing credit. They're stealing your oxygen. They're hijacking your comfort. They're weaponizing intimacy in the least romantic way possible.

And somehow, they think it's endearing. They think they're "approachable." They think this is good networking. But what they really are is the office equivalent of a pop-up ad you can't close.

Why They Do It (Fake Science Edition)

Close Proximity Disorder (CPD)

Symptoms: compulsive leaning, chronic breath-sharing, inappropriate hand pats.

Causes: childhood without personal bubbles, untreated extroversion, or mild sociopathy.

Prognosis: grim.

Treatment: repeated rejection, ideally via taser.

HR once tried to label it "engagement." The staff petitioned to rename it "oxygen theft."

The Toll on Your Sanity

Living with a Close Talker warps your sense of reality. You measure conversations in inches instead of minutes. You rehearse fake sneezes as evasive maneuvers. You wear headphones with no music just for plausible deniability.

Every shadow feels like an ambush. Every cough behind you is a prelude to proximity. Eventually, you stop making eye contact entirely, because eye contact is basically an engraved invitation.

Your therapist hears confessions like: "I dreamt Brian was standing in my fridge." You start keeping a tape measure at your desk. You fantasize about moving countries. You actually price witness protection.

Survival Strategies

The Step-Back Waltz: Each time they move in, you move back. Repeat until you've led them into the parking lot. Bonus: looks like you're auditioning for *Dancing With the Stars: HR Edition*.

Weaponize Furniture: Desks, chairs, plants — all become shields. A rolling chair is your riot gear. A tall ficus, your frontline. A standing desk? Your fortress tower.

The Pretend Cough: Their kryptonite. Nothing clears space faster than a post-pandemic hacking fit. Extra points if you mutter, "Doctor says it's still contagious."

The Eye Contact Blitz: Hold their gaze. No blink, no smile. Either they back off, or you accidentally create an HR case study.

The Direct Approach: Rare but effective. "Hey, can you step back? You're in my bubble." Watch as their brain blue-screens.

The Decoy Meeting: Block out your calendar with fake calls. When they lean in, gesture to your headset and whisper, "Sorry, client call."

The Ghosting Tactic: Pretend to take a phone call. Bonus if your ringtone is "Personal Space" by whoever you can bribe to write it.

Emergency Props
Hula hoop (boundary enforcement).
Open umbrella indoors (you'll look unhinged, but free).
Spray bottle (if it works for cats, why not Carl from IT?).
Noise-cancelling headphones (they'll still lean in, but at least you won't hear them breathe).
Fake hazmat suit. Call it "team spirit."

Bonus Activity: Close Talker Bingo

Breath fogged your glasses.
Backed you into a wall.
Whispered during a group conversation.
Lingering handshake.
Nose-to-nose dialogue.
"I'm not too close, am I?" while too close.
Hovered over your chair mid-meeting.
Blocked your only exit.
  Bingo! Your prize is a lungful of unshared air.

Why Justice Never Comes

Close Talkers are rarely punished. In fact, managers praise them.
  "They're so personable," they say. "So engaged."
  No. They're not personable. They're humid.
  Their behavior masquerades as enthusiasm. "Leaning in," managers call it, as if invading your lungs is a positive leadership trait. Only when a client complains — "Your employee tried to crawl

into my handbag while explaining an invoice" — does anyone realize it's not warmth, it's assault by proximity.

Until then, they roam unchecked, drifting from desk to desk like damp drones, sharing oxygen and unsolicited stories in equal measure.

Final Roast

So next time you're cornered by a Close Talker, don't panic. Remember: you're not the problem. They are.

They're not charismatic. They're not personable. They're not "good with people." They're space invaders in slacks. Pop-up ads without a close button.

And while they think they're beloved, what they're really building is a reputation as the office creep. They're the coworker new hires get warned about: "Watch out for Carl — he doesn't believe in personal space."

So laugh. Laugh as you sidestep like you're dodging a slow-motion bullet. Laugh as you barricade your cubicle with filing cabinets and ficus plants. Laugh because one day HR will finally get cornered in the copy room, and justice will be served.

Because clowns can juggle. But they'll never learn to count inches.

And when the Close Talker finally retires thinking they were "adored by the team," the real farewell party will be silent — just a collective deep breath. The first lungful of unshared oxygen in years.

Chapter Three
Meet Calamity Jane

Every office has a Calamity Jane. You don't hire her — she just *appears,* like glitter after a hen's night, impossible to get rid of and destined to linger forever. She's the coworker who shows up late, coffee in hand, eyeliner smudged from "just one glass" of wine that somehow lasted until 2 a.m.

Jane is a walking cautionary tale wrapped in a lanyard. She's never met a bad idea she didn't date, a round of shots she didn't accept, or a mechanical bull she couldn't conquer in heels. And yes, she *will* conquer it — right after she's spilled half her margarita on the marketing manager's new suede boots.

Her life philosophy? *"Too many yeses, not enough nos."* And she proves it daily. Yes to karaoke at the staff party. Yes to another tequila shot (at 10:47 p.m., on a work night). Yes to climbing on the company mascot after midnight because "it'll be hilarious." Yes to dating the IT contractor who still lives with his mum because he has "potential."

Calamity Jane is the reason HR sighs when they hear heels clattering down the hallway. She is chaos with a swipe card. A sitcom character in real life. A one-woman reality show that you didn't ask to be cast in but can't stop watching anyway.

And here's the thing: you *want* to hate her. You should hate her. But you don't. Because for all her mess, she's entertaining. Monday mornings are brighter because you get to hear how Jane "accidentally" ended up at a karaoke bar with the FedEx guy or why she was limping into work because "long story short... mechanical bull."

Jane doesn't just live life. She *crashes* into it, usually with sequins, bruises, and a hangover. And like any natural disaster, she's not preventable — you can only learn how to brace for impact.

The Classic Moves of Calamity Jane

If you're wondering how to spot a Calamity Jane in the wild, don't worry — she'll make herself known. She leaves a trail of chaos like glitter at a kid's birthday party. These are her signature classics:

1. The Late Entrance

Jane never just arrives. She *enters*. Usually fifteen to forty-five minutes late, armed with a coffee that smells suspiciously like it contains more Baileys than caffeine, and an excuse so elaborate it deserves an Oscar.

"You won't believe what happened..." she begins, launching into a tale involving a flat tyre, a neighbour's emergency, and a runaway dog — which somehow ends with her sitting at a traffic light crying to an Adele song.

By the time she's finished, she's charmed half the office into forgiving her and completely derailed the meeting agenda. The lateness isn't an accident; it's her brand.

2. The Boyfriend Disaster Tour

Every work function is a new episode of *Jane and the Terrible Plus-One*. She's brought the guy who hit on HR, the one who asked if the CEO's wife was "single," and the one who stole beers from the catering fridge.

Her taste in men is less "red flags" and more "entire emergency evacuation." And the kicker? She tells you, *every single time*, "I think he might be The One." Spoiler: he's not. He's just The One Who Will Cause HR to Draft an Incident Report.

3. The Volunteer Who Regrets

Jane has an Olympic-level talent for volunteering for things she will immediately regret. Sign-up sheet for the office fun run? She's there, even though the last time she jogged was to chase down a taco truck. Leading the Monday meeting? Sure, until she realizes she left her notes in the Uber.

Her enthusiasm is always pure — but watching her unravel halfway through is like watching a toddler promise to cook Thanksgiving dinner. You know it's going to end with tears, smoke, and someone calling for help.

4. The Party Legend

Jane isn't just part of the office Christmas party. She *is* the party. By 9 p.m., she's singing karaoke with the CFO. By 10, she's shot-gunning margaritas with the interns. By 11, she's somehow convinced someone to rent her a mechanical bull "because it would be hilarious."

And she rides it. In heels. For eight glorious seconds before gravity wins and Jane ends up sprawled on the floor, laughing louder than anyone else.

She drinks everyone under the table, then falls off it. And the next morning? She's in at 9:30, sunglasses on, claiming she feels "fresh as a daisy" while everyone else is still piecing together the photographic evidence.

5. The Morning After Promise

Every Calamity Jane has a catchphrase. Hers? *"I swear, I'll do better."*

She says it after showing up late. After oversharing in the lunchroom. After losing a shoe at the staff party. After riding the company mascot into the parking lot.

She never *does* better, of course. But the promise is part of the charm. Because deep down, you don't want her to change. The office needs its chaos agent. And Jane was built for the role.

How to Survive Calamity Jane

Living with Calamity Jane in your workplace isn't about preventing disaster — it's about *mitigating collateral damage*. She's less of a coworker and more of a natural phenomenon: you don't stop a hurricane; you just board up the windows and pray.

Here's how to keep your sanity intact:

1. Accept That Jane = Entertainment

Don't fight it. Monday morning meetings are instantly brighter when Jane breezes in late, eyeliner smudged, holding an iced latte and a story that starts with, *"So, there was this guy..."*

Her disasters are basically free Netflix. Sure, you'll never get that time back, but at least it's funny. Treat her chaos like your weekly sitcom episode: painful, dramatic, but impossible to look away from.

2. Never Agree to "Just One Drink"

Jane doesn't do "just one." She does *twelve*, plus karaoke, plus convincing you to try a flaming shot with a name that sounds like a dare.

You'll start the night thinking you're having a quiet beer after work, and end it holding her handbag while she challenges the bouncer to an arm-wrestle. The survival tactic here? *Say no. Always no.* Unless you want to spend your Friday night explaining to Uber why there's glitter in the backseat.

3. Keep HR's Number on Speed Dial

Where Jane goes, HR follows. Not because they want to, but because they have to. She's a walking case study in "What Not to Do at Work."

Pro tip: if you see her heading toward the karaoke machine with a tequila in one hand and a coworker's tie in the other, pre-dial HR. You'll save everyone time.

4. Plan Around Her Lateness

Treat Jane's calendar like weather forecasts. If the meeting starts at 9, assume she'll stroll in at 9:30 with an apology that involves flat tyres, traffic lights, and a pigeon that "looked injured" so she *had* to stop.

Schedule buffer time. Always. If you need her at noon, tell her 11:15. She'll still show up late, but closer to on time.

5. Contain the Chaos, Don't Cure It

You can't fix Jane. Therapy couldn't fix Jane. What you *can* do is contain her. Pair her with the one manager too boring to tolerate her antics. Sit her between two coworkers who will roll their eyes so hard she eventually quiets down.

Think of it like crowd control at a music festival. You don't stop the mosh pit — you just build barriers, so it doesn't spill into the carpark.

Bonus Activity: Calamity Jane Bingo

How do you know you've spent a night out with Calamity Jane? Easy — your camera roll is blurry, HR's inbox is full, and your dignity is missing.

Print this page, grab a pen, and play along at the next staff event. First to get a line wins the right to ghost Jane's next "just one drink" invite. Full house = automatic sick day.

Spills a drink on the boss
Shows up late but somehow stays the latest
Loses a shoe
Calls an ex before midnight
Rides something mechanical (bull, mascot, copier — anything will do)
Sings karaoke *without being asked*
Sings karaoke *twice*

Cries in the bathroom about "men these days"
Introduces a boyfriend of the week... who immediately hits on HR
Shouts "YOLO" unironically
Promises, *"I'll do better next time"*
Disappears for half an hour, returns covered in glitter
Posts a drunk Insta story tagging the company account
Starts a conga line in the wrong direction
Tries to ride the office mascot *again*
Claims she invented tequila
Wakes up with a mysterious bruise
Ends up in someone else's Uber
Demands the DJ play "her song"... three times
Monday morning: walks in late, says, *"You won't believe what happened."*

Why Justice Never Comes

Here's the cruel truth: Calamity Jane should've been fired ten times by now. HR has a bulging file with her name on it. She's been late more often than she's been on time, drunk more often than she's been sober at staff events, and has left more emotional wreckage in her wake than a bad season of *The Bachelor*.

And yet... she survives. Not only survives — sometimes *thrives*.

Because in the twisted logic of office life, Jane's chaos gets rebranded as "fun." She's not reckless — she's "the life of the party." She's not unprofessional — she's "relatable." She's not chronically late — she's "fashionably delayed."

When she stumbles into Monday's meeting in sunglasses and an oversized latte, you see a hungover liability. Management? They see "someone who brings energy to the team." Energy! This is a woman who once tried to ride the inflatable snowman at the Christmas party.

Jane has mastered the art of survival by being too entertaining to let go. HR sighs, managers roll their eyes, but everyone else secretly roots for her — because no one wants to sit through a staff party without Jane's antics. She's chaos, yes, but she's *good TV*.

The only time consequences even *threaten* to arrive is when she pushes it too far in front of clients. Like the infamous night she introduced her "boyfriend" (met him on Tinder 48 hours earlier) to the regional director, and he spent twenty minutes asking if the company had an employee discount on laptops.

Even then, Jane wriggled out of it. She laughed, charmed, and turned the whole thing into a story the director now tells at conferences. That's Jane's true gift: transforming disaster into legend.

So justice? It never comes. HR knows better than to try. Jane is inevitable. Jane is eternal. Jane is the reason "code of conduct" policies have so many pages.

Final Roast

You don't *manage* a Calamity Jane. You don't mentor her, discipline her, or coach her into "better choices." You simply strap in, hang on, and hope the HR department has enough liability waivers on file.

Because Jane isn't a coworker. She's a walking season finale. She's tequila in human form. She's chaos in heels, carrying a handbag full of regret and a phone full of exes she *will* text before midnight.

She thinks she's building relationships, living her best life, and "keeping things fun." What she's really building is a trail of glitter, broken glass, and HR paperwork that will outlast civilizations. Archaeologists could dig up your office in 500 years and still find Jane's sequins buried in the carpet.

And yet, somehow, you'll miss her when she's gone. Because while she leaves you exhausted, late on deadlines, and wondering how she hasn't been fired yet — she also leaves you with the best Monday morning stories of your career.

So laugh. Laugh when she stumbles into the meeting half an hour late with one shoe missing. Laugh when she climbs the company mascot like it's her personal Everest. Laugh because when HR finally reaches their breaking point, you'll be the one telling future interns: *"Oh, you should've been here when we had a Calamity Jane."*

Because clowns can juggle. But only Jane can juggle bad men, bad tequila, and bad decisions — and still walk in Monday morning claiming she's "fresh as a daisy."

Chapter Four
The Weird Smell Guy

Eau de Office Horror

Every office has one. You don't need to see him to know he's arrived — your nose does the job for you. He is the **Weird Smell Guy**, the coworker whose very existence is less about productivity and more about *olfactory assault*.

And if you're sitting there smugly thinking, *"We don't have one in our office,"* then congratulations: it's probably you.

Weird Smell Guy is not defined by one scent. No, that would almost be merciful. He is a kaleidoscope of odors, a walking chemistry experiment, an ever-changing buffet of smells that range from *"vaguely unpleasant"* to *"dear God, my nostrils are on fire."*

Monday: The Eternal Gym Bag

On Mondays, he wafts in carrying the stale musk of gym clothes that clearly never made it into the washing machine. You can practically hear the bacteria holding a rave in his socks. He insists he went to the gym "late last night," but judging by the smell, those sneakers last saw soap during the Obama administration.

He drops his duffel bag under the desk, and within minutes the entire row is Googling *"How long does athlete's foot survive on carpet?"*

Tuesday: The Eggpocalypse

Tuesday is protein day. Weird Smell Guy cracks open a Tupperware of boiled eggs — sometimes plain, sometimes lovingly paired with blue cheese or tuna. He strolls to the communal microwave at 9:15 a.m. sharp, presses start, and within seconds the office air turns hostile.

By the time the microwave dings, the building doesn't smell like productivity anymore. It smells like a biology experiment that escaped its jar.

Wednesday: The Cologne Catastrophe

By Wednesday, he's trying to fix it. And by "fix it," I mean drown it in cologne. Not a spritz, either — half a bottle of something called *Wolf Predator 3000*. Suddenly the office smells like a nightclub bathroom at 3 a.m. — a potent cocktail of cheap cologne, despair, and broken dreams.

The combination of Tuesday's egg funk and today's overcompensating spray creates a hybrid odor scientists could weaponize if they weren't already gagging.

Thursday: The Garlic Gambit

Thursday is garlic. Always garlic. It seeps out of his pores, clings to his keyboard, and lingers in meeting rooms long after he's gone. You know it's bad when even the whiteboard markers start to smell like garlic bread.

When he leans over your desk to ask about the quarterly figures, it feels like Dracula's revenge. You're not collaborating; you're surviving.

Friday: The Mystery Funk

And then comes Friday. The grand finale. Nobody knows what causes it. Is it unwashed laundry? Is it last night's pub crawl leaking through his skin? Is it... something darker? Theories abound, but one thing is certain: Friday Funk isn't natural. It's the kind of smell that makes you question your life choices, your career, and whether nostril hair was actually a good evolutionary idea.

The Seasonal Doom

In summer, it's swamp. Sweat, sunscreen, and polyester shirts fermenting into one sticky haze. Winter? Wet wool and damp shoes, a smell that clings to the office carpet like mildew in an old basement.

Spring should be hopeful — flowers, fresh air — but not with Weird Smell Guy. Spring means pollen mixing with his "natural musk" until your sinuses beg for a transfer. Autumn is worse: the earthy stench of fallen leaves somehow fuses with whatever spice cloud he's discovered that week. Pumpkin spice, cumin, cinnamon — comforting in a café, horrifying when blended with B.O. at 9 a.m.

Every season is a new torment. The calendar doesn't measure months anymore. It measures phases of his stink.

The Curse of Open Plan

If you're lucky, Weird Smell Guy sits at the far end of the office, contained within his own miasma. If you're unlucky, he's a desk buddy. Which means his aura becomes *your* aura. Clients walk in, sniff the air, and suddenly your whole team looks guilty.

And in the cruel democracy of open-plan design, there's nowhere to hide. The smell travels. It spreads. It seeps through partitions, across hallways, into your very soul. You can't escape him. You can only marinate in him.

The Niceness Trap

Here's the kicker: he's often... nice. Too nice. He's polite, he brings muffins, he remembers your birthday. Which makes it impossible to confront him. You can't exactly say, *"Thanks for the banana bread, Dave, but your scent profile is melting my corneas."*

You suffer in silence, forced to smile and nod while he tells you about his weekend hiking trip — a story that smells like damp socks and petrol.

The Office Ghost

Even when he's not there, he's there. His absence isn't marked by quiet — it's marked by lingering smell. You walk into a meeting room and immediately know he was there earlier. It's like walking into a haunted house, but instead of ghosts it's eau de microwaved trout.

People leave Post-it notes on the door: *"DON'T GO IN."* But it's too late. You've already inhaled.

The Tragedy of Desensitization

Here's the real tragedy: after a while, you stop noticing. The human brain, desperate for survival, numbs itself to the constant assault. Until one day you leave the office, meet a friend for drinks, and they wrinkle their nose and say: *"Why do you smell like reheated fish and Axe body spray?"*

Congratulations. You've been contaminated.

The Classic Moves of Weird Smell Guy

Every office has endured the greatest hits of his scent symphony. Here are the ones that turn him from "slightly whiffy" into a full-blown office legend.

The Elevator Trap
The doors slide shut. You're alone. He's there. Within seconds, the air is thick with his "signature scent." You press every button in panic just to escape on the next floor, but it's too late — the damage is done. Your jacket now smells like him. Forever.

The Sweaty Handshake
Somehow always damp, always clammy, and always offered with unearned confidence. You don't just shake his hand — you adopt his sweat. It lingers on your palm like a curse until you're scrubbing in the bathroom like you've witnessed a crime scene.

The Scented Sit-Down
He leaves the chair. You sit down after him. Instantly regret it. The seat cushion is warm *and* smelly, radiating a funk that clings to your trousers like a bad tattoo. You now smell like his lower back for the rest of the day. Congratulations.

The Phantom Stink
Sometimes, the smell isn't even him. But he's built such a reputation that every mystery odor in the office is pinned on Weird Smell Guy. Microwave explodes with burnt popcorn? Must be

him. Funky smell near the printer? Definitely him. Even when he's on annual leave, people still say, *"Smells like Dave's here."*

The Meeting Room Biohazard

He shows up late to a meeting, takes the seat right in the middle, and within minutes the smell has spread wall-to-wall. By the end, people aren't just discussing budgets — they're calculating how much they'd pay to never breathe through their nose again.

The Sweat print

Hot day? He leaves behind sweat marks on chairs, keyboards, or — God forbid — shared equipment. The office reacts like archaeologists discovering a fossil: pointing, photographing, documenting. HR pretends not to notice, but Facilities files a quiet work order to replace the upholstery.

The "Natural Products" Disaster

In a rare attempt to fix things, he switches to "all-natural deodorant." Which works about as well as a paper umbrella in a hurricane. The result: earthy funk layered with B.O. so raw it could be bottled and sold as *regret*.

The Overtime Aura

By 6 p.m., when everyone else smells like mild fatigue, Weird Smell Guy smells like an entire week condensed into one man. It's not B.O. anymore — it's a life choice. Stay late with him and you'll discover what despair really smells like.

The Toll on Your Sanity

Working with Weird Smell Guy is less like having a coworker and more like being trapped in an ongoing sensory experiment nobody consented to. It doesn't just test your patience — it tests your very will to live.

Every day becomes a game of *"What fresh hell awaits my nostrils today?"* You sit down at your desk, coffee in hand, and before you even log in, you smell it. Is it gym socks? Is it last night's vindaloo reheated for breakfast? Is it a cologne so aggressive it could double as pepper spray?

You'll never know until it's too late.

The Silent Suffering

The worst part is that nobody wants to be the one to say it out loud. Everyone smells it. Everyone's suffering. But confronting Weird Smell Guy feels like kicking a puppy. He's not mean. He's not malicious. He's just... olfactorily offensive. So instead, the office collectively chooses silent misery.

Colleagues swap looks in meetings, pinch their noses discreetly, and text each other under the table: *"Is it just me or is it garlic day again?"* It's like living in a hostage situation, only the captor is blissfully unaware.

The Contamination Effect

Proximity is dangerous. Sit too close, and his aura clings to you like secondhand smoke. You'll leave the office smelling faintly of him, which means *you* get the side-eye on the train home. You can try to explain, but how do you tell a stranger, *"It's not me, it's my coworker Dave"* without sounding insane?

The Meeting Room Nightmare

Nothing breaks your spirit faster than being trapped in a sealed meeting room with him. Air-conditioning doesn't help. Open windows don't help. After ten minutes, everyone is less focused on strategy and more focused on survival. People start volunteering to "grab printouts" just to get a breath of hallway air. By the end, the meeting notes are illegible because the scribe's tears blurred the ink.

The Workplace Gaslighting

He doesn't notice. He thinks he smells fine. Worse — he thinks he smells *good*. He'll saunter past your desk after drenching himself in "Ocean Thunder" body spray and say, *"Got a new cologne. Pretty sharp, hey?"* Meanwhile, you're choking back bile and wondering if "sharp" is his word for "acidic assault."

The Seasonal Doom

In summer, it's sweat. In winter, it's wet wool. Autumn, he leans into pumpkin-spiced disaster. Spring, pollen mixes with his natural musk until your sinuses file for divorce. Every season brings a new torment. The calendar doesn't measure time anymore. It measures phases of his stink.

The Emotional Whiplash

Weird Smell Guy breaks you down slowly. At first, you laugh. Then you complain. Then you stop complaining. Finally, you accept it as your new reality. This is the *Stockholm Syndrome of smell*. One day, you'll find yourself defending him: *"Yeah, it's bad, but at least today it's just curry."* That's not acceptance. That's resignation.

Living with his scent cloud doesn't just damage your nose. It damages your soul. By Friday, you're less an employee and more a survivor, clutching your Febreze like a holy relic and praying for the weekend.

Survival Guide: How to Endure Weird Smell Guy

You can't cure him. You can't fix him. You can only build defenses, minimize exposure, and pray your nostrils survive another quarter. Here's your step-by-step disaster plan:

1. The Layered Scarf Strategy

Always keep a scarf, hoodie, or oversized cardigan on hand. Not for fashion — for survival. One whiff of his tuna curry, and you've got an instant nose barrier. Bonus: muffled laughter when your coworkers see you rocking "biohazard chic."

2. The Febreze Under the Desk

Forget filing cabinets — your most valuable office supply is a spray bottle of air freshener hidden in your bottom drawer. Deploy it discreetly when he walks past, but pace yourself. Too much, and you'll asphyxiate yourself before he does.

3. The Coffee Cup Shield

Keep a steaming cup of coffee under your nose at all times. Sip strategically. Not because you need the caffeine (though you do), but because coffee steam is the only thing standing between you and Eau de Gym Bag.

4. The Strategic Relocation

Claim you "need more natural light" or "have to sit closer to the printer." Translation: you need to move away from his aura before it permanently embeds itself in your DNA. HR will nod sympathetically. They know.

5. The Meeting Sacrifice

If you get stuck in a room with him, rotate "sacrifices." Don't take the hit every time. Assign someone else to sit next to him — rotate like jury duty. Nobody wants it, but fairness matters in survival situations.

6. The Elevator Escape Plan
Never enter an elevator with him alone. If you're already trapped, fake a phone call, press every button, or dramatically "forget something" on another floor. You may look crazy, but at least you'll smell sane.

7. The Candle Conspiracy
Convince the office manager that scented candles are "great for morale." Place them strategically around the office. If Weird Smell Guy asks why the office smells like lavender instead of his leftover mackerel pie, shrug and say it's "team culture."

8. The Gas Mask Fantasy
You'll never wear it — but imagining yourself walking into Monday's meeting with a full hazmat mask is sometimes the only thing that gets you through.

Survival isn't about winning. It's about not dying inside every time he reheats fish curry at 9:15 a.m. Because let's face it: Weird Smell Guy isn't going anywhere. His scent is forever.

Why Justice Never Comes

Here's the unbearable truth: Weird Smell Guy should've been stopped years ago. HR should've sat him down. Management should've intervened. Somebody — anybody — should've handed him deodorant, detergent, or at least a polite note that said *"please stop microwaving seafood at 9 a.m."*

But nope. Nothing.

Because the office doesn't run on fairness. It runs on avoidance. And avoiding conflict is easier than telling Dave he smells like a compost heap stuffed with regret.

So instead of justice, here's what happens:

HR waves it away with: *"We don't want to embarrass him."* Meanwhile, the rest of you are embarrassed every time a client wrinkles their nose.

Management calls him "authentic" or "a real character," as if being a biohazard is somehow endearing.

Colleagues whisper and text under the table, but never confront.

And so, Weird Smell Guy thrives. Not because he's competent. Not because he's talented. But because smelling like despair isn't technically against policy.

Final Roast

The Weird Smell Guy is not just a coworker. He's an atmosphere. A force of nature. A weather system of funk that HR can't measure and management refuses to acknowledge.

You can't fire him — because technically, he hasn't broken a rule. You can't confront him — because technically, "smelling like a tuna curry wrapped in wet wool" isn't in the employee handbook. So he endures.

And while you fantasize about transferring floors, switching jobs, or installing industrial fans under your desk, Weird Smell Guy just keeps floating along. Oblivious. Cheerful. Offering you gum from a pocket that smells like garlic death.

He will outlast you. He will outlast the CEO, the interns, even the office furniture. Long after you've gone, his scent will be etched into the upholstery like nicotine in a dive bar. New hires will sit down and whisper, *"Smells like Dave's still here."*

So laugh. Laugh when he cracks open leftover eggs at 9 a.m. Laugh when he leaves a chair smelling like despair. Laugh when his "signature scent" follows you into the elevator and ruins your lunch appetite. Because what else can you do?

Because clowns can juggle, sure. But Weird Smell Guy? He can juggle sweat, garlic, eggs, and cologne — all at once — and still look you dead in the eye, wondering why you're holding your breath.

Chapter Five
The Career Olympian

Welcome to the Corporate Games

The Career Olympian doesn't just show up to work. They compete.

Every day is a race, every meeting is a qualifying round, and every hallway chat with management is a gold-medal opportunity. While you're still booting up your laptop, they've already visualized themselves on the podium, arms raised, bathing in imaginary applause.

They talk about "playing the long game," but let's be real: they're playing *every* game, all at once. To them, you're not a coworker — you're a hurdle, a lap marker, or an obstacle course in their personal corporate decathlon.

The 100-Meter Suck-Up

The Career Olympian has a supernatural ability to appear every time the boss walks by. One moment they're nowhere, the next they're materializing beside the coffee machine like they teleported in, blurting out:

"Oh, I was *just* thinking about that initiative too!"

It's not coincidence. It's training. Their stopwatch is synced to the boss's footsteps, and they never miss the chance to sprint into the spotlight.

The Email Marathon

You go home at 5:30. The Olympian? They're just getting warmed up. At 11:47 p.m., your phone buzzes with a message stamped *"Sent from my iPhone"* (always that humblebrag footer). It's about "strategic opportunities" nobody asked for.

By morning, your inbox is clogged with essays masquerading as updates. Every project has been hijacked, every idea rebranded as something they've been "pushing for." This isn't communication. It's performance art in Outlook.

The PowerPoint Pentathlon

For the Olympian, a slide deck isn't a tool — it's an arena. Their presentation style has five predictable events:

Unnecessary animations that make charts spin like carnival rides.

Stock photos of people laughing at salads.

Fonts that change mid-slide for no reason.

Buzzwords delivered at world-record pace.

A closing quote from Steve Jobs. Always Steve Jobs.

By the end, management claps like they've just seen a TED Talk. You're left wondering how you got trapped in a slideshow triathlon of doom.

The LinkedIn High Jump

If they don't post about it, did it even happen? The Career Olympian treats LinkedIn like their personal Olympic broadcast. Every minor task becomes a #LeadershipMoment. Every half-baked brainstorm becomes a #VisionForTheFuture. You'll scroll past their updates at night, teeth grinding, as they thank the "amazing team" for work they didn't even touch.

The Podium Pose

You know it's coming. That chest-out, chin-up stance when the boss praises *their* "initiative." Never mind that you built the spreadsheet, ran the data, and drafted the deck. The Olympian beams like they've just smashed a world record. They might even go for the fake-humble, *"Oh, it was really a team effort."* Sure. A team effort where they grabbed the medal and shoved everyone else off the stage.

The Eternal Training Montage

While normal people enjoy weekends, the Career Olympian spends them networking, rehearsing pitches, and listening to podcasts about productivity hacks. Monday morning, they'll regale you with tales of "maximizing efficiency" while you're still trying to remember your password. Their whole life is a Rocky-style training montage, except instead of running up stairs, they're practicing PowerPoint transitions.

The result? You can't keep up. You *shouldn't* keep up. Because unlike you — a human being who values lunch breaks, personal space, and sanity — the Career Olympian has one goal: **promotion at any cost.**

And if that means sacrificing your peace, stealing your ideas, or turning every goddamn team huddle into a medal ceremony? So be it.

Because in their mind, they're not just climbing the ladder. They're *winning the Games.*

The Classic Moves of the Career Olympian

The Classic Moves of the Career Olympian

Spotting a Career Olympian is easy. They can't resist turning the smallest office moment into their personal gold-medal performance.

The Name-Drop Vault

You're having a normal conversation about lunch when suddenly they vault into it:

"Yeah, I was just talking to Karen from the executive suite about that yesterday."

Karen is the CFO. You were talking about sandwiches.

The Olympian drops names like confetti, hoping management overhears and assumes they're part of the inner circle.

The Elevator Sprint

They time their arrivals and exits with Olympic precision. Somehow, they always end up alone in the elevator with the boss. By the time the doors open, they've pitched three "strategic visions" and a half-baked product idea. You were in the same meeting last week when they stayed silent. Weird coincidence.

The Resume Gymnastics

Their CV reads less like a career and more like a Marvel origin story.

"Project Lead" becomes "Global Strategic Visionary."

"Wrote meeting notes" becomes "Chief Knowledge Architect."

They'll italicize, bold, and trademark anything if it makes their bullet points look shinier.

The Agenda Hurdle

Every meeting has an agenda — until the Olympian shows up. Suddenly it's derailed:

"That's great, but what if we redirected resources into my innovative side project?"

Congratulations. Your quarterly review is now the Carl Show.

The Networking Decathlon

Conferences are their Olympics. While you're still finding the coffee cart, they've already shaken twenty hands, taken thirty selfies, and collected forty LinkedIn connections. By Monday morning, their recap email makes it sound like they negotiated world peace — over canapés.

The Hackathon Hurdle

Company announces an "innovation sprint"? They sprint to sign up. Do they code? No. Do they contribute? Only if you count rearranging sticky notes into motivational shapes. But by the end, they're front and center in the group photo, thanking the team for "pioneering solutions." Their biggest innovation was finding the best lighting for the photographer.

The Buzzword Weightlifting

They measure strength in jargon per minute. "Synergize scalable frameworks to leverage paradigm shifts" — that's their personal best. By the time they finish a sentence, you're crushed under the weight of all the empty words.

The Applause Rehearsal

Ever notice how they pause dramatically mid-presentation? That's not nerves. That's practice. They're leaving space for applause that never comes. And if nobody claps, don't worry — they'll clap for themselves.

The Sabotage Stretch

They'll casually "forget" to tell you about a deadline. Then, at the last minute, they swoop in with the fix, looking like the hero while you look like the slacker. It's not teamwork. It's sabotage with extra stretching.

The Olympic Torch of Gossip

When all else fails, they light up the rumor mill. Did they hear that promotion was already decided? Oh yes. Did they hear the VP "loved" their presentation? Absolutely. Are any of these things true? About as true as their "Global Strategic Visionary" title.

The Toll on Your Sanity

Working near a Career Olympian is like being trapped in a never-ending motivational montage — except you're not Rocky, you're the punching bag. Their relentless energy isn't inspiring. It's exhausting.

Every day you're forced to watch them sprint, vault, and cartwheel their way up the corporate ladder while you're just trying to finish your coffee before it goes cold. It doesn't matter what you achieve, because the Olympian will always spin it as part of their highlight reel. Slowly, it wears you down.

The Ego Fog

Spend too much time around them, and you start to feel smaller. It's not just their ambition — it's their volume. They talk longer, louder, and with more conviction than anyone else in the room. Even when they're spectacularly wrong, people nod along just to get it over with. Meanwhile, you're left with bruises from the secondhand smug.

The Constant Comparison

Your boss doesn't mean to, but it happens. "Look how driven Carl is — maybe you could take a page from his book?" Sure. If the book is titled *How to Be an Obnoxious, Credit-Stealing Ladder Goblin,* maybe. Suddenly, your healthy work-life balance looks lazy next to their 14-hour days and LinkedIn humblebrags.

The Career Hunger Games

They turn everything into a competition. Who came in earliest? Who used the most jargon in a meeting? Who can send the latest email at night? It's never collaboration — always combat. And if you're not playing their game, you're automatically losing. Which is insane, because you never signed up.

The Silent Rage

You'll never snap. You'll never scream. You'll never tell them to shut up about their "vision for the company." But you will grind your teeth so hard at night your dentist will ask if you're stress-chewing bricks. The Olympian doesn't just drain your energy — they infest your nervous system.

The Emotional Endurance Test

Working with them isn't work. It's survival training. You don't clock in; you enter an arena. And the only medal you'll ever get is the one you award yourself for surviving another day in their orbit without flipping a table.

Survival Guide: Outrunning the Career Olympian

You can't stop them. You can't reason with them. You can only build strategies to protect your sanity while they vault over your dignity. Here's how to survive their endless Corporate Games:

1. The Paper Trail Podium

Always email your ideas before a meeting. Copy the whole team. Hell, copy Facilities. That way, when the Olympian tries to sprint off with your brilliance, you've already planted your flag like a corporate land grabber.

2. The Strategic Clapback

When they parrot your idea louder and slower, smile sweetly and say:
"Yes, just like I mentioned earlier."
Do it often enough and you'll see their Olympic grin twitch like they just pulled a hamstring.

3. The Decoy Project

Feed them a shiny, doomed-to-fail idea. Watch them run with it like it's the cure for cancer. Sit back with popcorn as they pitch it to management, only to trip over their own buzzwords. Congratulations — you've just handed them a bronze in humiliation.

4. The Praise Pivot

When the boss thanks the Olympian for "leading the way," immediately thank them for "building on your work." It's subtle. It's polite. But it's the verbal equivalent of tripping them mid-sprint.

5. The Meeting Shield

Always sit between them and management. Become the human hurdle. If they want to launch into another medal-ceremony monologue, they have to physically lean over you to do it. Bonus: front-row access to their flop sweat.

6. The Boundary Marathon

Never compete on their terms. Don't stay until midnight. Don't spam emails at 3 a.m. Don't adopt their buzzwords just to fit in. Guard your boundaries like Olympic records. Because unlike them, you'd rather win at life.

7. The LinkedIn Block

Do yourself a favor: mute them. Their inspirational posts about "grit" and "visionary leadership" will only fuel your rage. Out of sight, out of blood-pressure spike.

8. The Escape Plan

If all else fails, remember: Olympians burn out. They run too hard, too fast, too loud. Eventually, they sprint into a wall of their own bullshit. Your job is simple: survive long enough to watch it happen.

Why Justice Never Comes

Here's the cruel truth: Career Olympians almost always get rewarded. Not because they're brilliant. Not because they're innovative. But because management mistakes shamelessness for leadership.

They don't get called out for hijacking meetings — they get praised for being "confident."

They don't get in trouble for stealing credit — they're "strategic thinkers."

They don't get roasted for staying until midnight — they're "dedicated."

Everything they do gets reframed as ambition, not annoyance.

The Perception Podium

While you're grinding through real work, they're polishing their medal pose. While you're stressing over deadlines, they're rehearsing inspirational quotes for the performance review. And the boss eats it up.

The Olympian doesn't just survive in corporate life — they thrive. Promotions fall into their lap. Awards get handed to them. They collect LinkedIn endorsements like Pokémon cards. And all the while, the rest of the office mutters under their breath, silently screaming:

"But they don't do anything!"

The System Rewards Noise

It doesn't matter. Because Career Olympians understand something most people don't: in corporate life, perception beats reality. They don't need to be the best. They just need to *look* like the best long enough to outshine you.

Noise gets noticed. Noise gets rewarded. And nobody makes more noise than someone sprinting up the ladder with both hands full of buzzwords.

The Eventual Faceplant

But take comfort. Career Olympians eventually get too high, too fast, too visible. And when that happens? They're asked to actually deliver. Suddenly there's no one left to steal from. No one left to blame. No one left to run over.

That's when the gold medalist trips on their own ego and face-plants on the corporate track. Watching that slow-motion collapse? That's the closest thing to justice you'll ever get.

Final Roast

Here's the thing about Career Olympians: they think they're winning. They strut through the office like champions, flashing their smug little podium pose every time the boss nods their way. They live for the applause, the titles, the hollow victories etched into their résumés in 16-point bold.

But everyone else? We're not impressed. We see the shortcuts. We hear the buzzwords. We watch them vault over teamwork, sprint past accountability, and pole-vault into middle management on nothing but ego fumes.

The Hollow Victories

Sure, they'll collect their promotions. They'll rack up their LinkedIn trophies. They'll bask in the glow of every performance review where they "exceeded expectations" by doing little more than running their mouths. But here's the truth they can't outrun: clowns don't stay champions forever.

Eventually, the lights dim. The crowd stops clapping. The boss leans in and says:
"Okay. Now actually lead."

And that's when the whole act collapses. The buzzwords dry up. The fake enthusiasm wilts. The medals rust. And suddenly, the office realizes what you've known all along — this wasn't a champion. This was just a wannabe athlete in a cheap suit, juggling jargon and calling it victory.

The Real Winner

So laugh. Laugh every time they pause in a presentation waiting for applause that never comes. Laugh when they sprint past you like it's the goddamn Olympics. Laugh because one day, their race will end.

And when it does? You'll still be there — sipping your coffee, minding your business, and enjoying the sweetest victory of all: not caring.

Because clowns can juggle, sure. But they can't run forever.

Chapter Six

Meet Pill-Popping Penny

MEET PILL-POPPING PENNY

Some coworkers run on coffee. Some run on sheer willpower. And then there's Penny. Pill-Popping Penny. The human embodiment of a pharmacy clearance bin, singlehandedly putting the *big* in Big Pharma.

She's single, desperate, and fueled entirely by prescription "pick-me-ups." Anxiety meds, diet pills, mystery capsules she swears are "all-natural." If it comes in blister packs, Penny's on it. Her handbag rattles like a maraca when she walks.

Penny doesn't just take the edge off — she files it down to dust. She drifts through the office in a haze of artificial calm, punctuated by sudden bursts of manic energy that suggest the pills have kicked in a little *too* hard.

One day she's sobbing at her desk because a client "used the wrong tone." The next she's bouncing off the walls, reorganizing the supply cabinet at warp speed. She is chaos, but pharmaceutical-grade chaos.

And yet, despite it all, Penny has stories. Legendary stories. Like the time she phoned you from the desk five yards away to whisper, *"I can't stand up. You need to help me get to the café."*

Turns out, the pills she'd popped for "stress" had done their job a little too well. She needed you to come over, let her lean on you like a drunk bridesmaid, and escort her across the office floor — past all your colleagues — just so she could eat a muffin and "soak up the meds."

Because her legs gave way before your standards did.

Penny isn't just a coworker. She's an office legend. A cautionary tale wrapped in a prescription label. And the reason HR now includes *"Please don't abuse pharmaceuticals"* in their annual compliance training.

The Classic Moves of Pill-Popping Penny

1. The Desk-Drawer Dispensary
Most people keep pens and Post-its in their drawer. Penny? She runs a pharmacy out of hers. Rattling pill bottles, half-empty blister packs, and mystery capsules that look like they came from an unlicensed chemist in Bali. Open her drawer and it sounds like 10,000 tik taks.

2. The Monday Morning Collapse
Every Monday she staggers in with fresh stories of heartbreak, poor choices, and "bad reactions." She'll sigh dramatically, flop into her chair, and explain how "this weekend was *different*." It never is.

3. The Lunchtime "Just One"
For Penny, lunch isn't about food. It's about "balancing her levels." Out comes a mysterious blister pack, she swallows "just one," and spends the afternoon either reorganizing the filing cabinet like a speed demon or face-planted on her desk drooling on HR's policy manual.

4. The Overshare Hour
Penny doesn't just tell you about her love life. She narrates it in *graphic detail*. By 11 a.m. you know more about her date's dietary issues than you do about your own family. And if she's mid-pill swing? Buckle up — the monologue will last longer than most of her relationships.

5. The Staff-Party Meltdown
Cocktails + pharmaceuticals = the Penny special. By 9 p.m., she's hugging strangers. By 10, she's crying about "never finding real love." By 11, she's belting out Total Eclipse Of The Heart into a shoe she's mistaken for a microphone. HR doesn't even bother writing up her party behavior anymore. It's all in a file just called *Penny*.

The Toll on Your Sanity

Working with Penny isn't work. It's emotional CrossFit. Every hour is a new round of chaos, and you never know which version of Penny is going to show up.

One morning she's bouncing off the walls, rearranging the supply closet and telling you about her "exciting new side hustle" selling essential oils. The next, she's curled in her chair under a blanket, whispering about how life is meaningless and asking if you'd walk with her to the café because "she can't feel her legs."

It's exhausting. Not because you care (you stopped caring somewhere around meltdown #12), but because she drags you into the performance whether you want to participate or not.

You try to type an email, and Penny's leaning across your desk with:

"Do you think it's weird if a guy brings his mum on a second date?"

You try to eat lunch, and she's pulling a mystery pill from her handbag, asking if you think "it'll react badly with wine."

You try to get through a meeting, and she interrupts with a dramatic sigh loud enough to make the CEO ask if "everything's okay over there." Spoiler: it's never okay.

And the cycle never ends. You're not just her coworker; you're her unwilling therapist, pill-checker, relationship coach, and designated lifter-upper when her legs give out.

Over time, you develop survival instincts. You stop making eye contact. You pretend to be on urgent calls. You wear headphones with no music playing, just so you can dodge her monologues about her "emotional breakthroughs."

But even with all that, Penny still gets under your skin. Because deep down, you know that when she spirals — and she always spirals — you're going to be the one stuck holding her handbag, escorting her to HR, or Googling, *"How many Xanax is too many?"*

Penny doesn't just wear down your patience. She wears down your very will to participate in office life. And by the end of each week, you find yourself wondering: *Is she chaotic because of the pills... or are the pills just trying to keep up with her chaos?*

Survival Guide: How to Outlive Pill-Popping Penny

Let's be real: you can't fix Penny. She's not a problem to be solved — she's a storm to be weathered. Your best hope is to protect yourself, build defensive systems, and pray you're not on her shortlist of "emergency contacts."

Here's your survival playbook:

1. The Emergency Exit Plan

Always know your escape routes. If Penny approaches with that glassy look in her eye and a mystery pill halfway to her mouth, you need options: the bathroom, the stairwell, or, in extreme cases, the fire alarm.

2. The Headphone Barrier

Noise-cancelling headphones aren't for music. They're for Penny. Slip them on, nod occasionally, and pretend you're listening to a motivational podcast. She'll assume you're "super busy" and find another victim to unload her drama onto.

Advanced tactic: keep the cord unplugged. That way you can still hear her, but at least she *thinks* you're ignoring her.

3. The Lunch Shift

Never — and I mean *never* — sit next to Penny at lunch. She will either:

a) produce a fistful of mystery pills like a magician pulling scarves out of a hat, or

b) narrate her most recent Tinder disaster between bites of salad.

Your best move is to take lunch early, late, or anywhere within a three-block radius of the office.

4. The Strategic Deflection

If Penny corners you, change the subject to something boring enough to derail her energy. Spreadsheets. Compliance policies. Printer toner. She'll glaze over and wander off in search of a more stimulating victim.

5. The HR Buffer Zone

Keep HR on speed dial. Not to report her (they already have her entire file color-coded), but to use them as a shield. If she's spiraling, drop a casual, *"You know who would love to hear about this? HR."* Then walk away while she diverts toward the professionals.

6. The Pharmaceutical Bingo

Keep a secret bingo card in your desk:

"These are just vitamins."

"It's fine, my doctor's cool with it."

"I just need one little pick-me-up."

"Can you help me stand?"

"This is the *last* time, I swear."

Five in a row = permission to leave work early.

7. The Nuclear Option: Relocation

If all else fails, request a desk move. Tell Facilities you're "seeking more natural light" or "need to be closer to the printer." Don't admit it's because Penny keeps asking if she can "just lean on you for a sec." Pack your plants, grab your stapler, and run like you're escaping a cult.

Surviving Penny isn't about thriving. It's about minimizing the damage, rationing your patience, and keeping your sanity intact until 5 p.m. Because the only cure for Penny is... retirement. Hers, not yours.

Why Justice Never Comes

Here's the maddening truth: Pill-Popping Penny should've been escorted out of the building years ago. She's called in "sick" more times than she's shown up sober, cried in more meetings than she's contributed to, and her desk drawer has more controlled substances than a pharmacy raid.

And yet... she's still here.

Why? Because Penny has mastered the art of weaponized fragility. The bosses don't see a walking disaster — they see a *delicate soul*. A "sensitive spirit" who just "needs a little extra support." HR doesn't discipline her because, frankly, they don't want the paperwork. Easier to let her coast than to deal with the fallout when she collapses mid-warning.

Penny's chaos even gets rebranded as charm. "She's quirky," they say. "She's eccentric." Translation: she's high as a kite but somehow still turns in her expense reports.

The closest she's ever come to consequences was the infamous staff party incident where she sang power ballads into her shoe. Management? They laughed. HR? They sighed. Penny? She shrugged and promised, *"I'll do better."* And by Monday, everyone had moved on — except you, because you were the one holding her handbag while she wept about how "men don't understand her."

Justice doesn't touch Penny. It tiptoes around her, afraid she'll cry, collapse, or call HR herself to complain about "lack of support."

So she keeps her job, keeps her paycheck, and keeps rattling into work every Monday like a human pillbox on wheels.

Because in the twisted ecosystem of office life, Penny isn't a liability — she's "a character." And as long as people are entertained, nobody cares about the pharmaceutical circus she's running from her desk.

Final Roast

Here's the truth about Penny: she's not a colleague; she's a cautionary tale with a lanyard. She thinks she's surviving the corporate grind, but really, she's surviving on blister packs and blind luck.

She believes she's "coping." What she's really doing is creating an HR horror anthology — one pill, one overshare, one meltdown at a time. Every Monday morning, every staff party, every shaky walk to the café adds another chapter to her legend.

And while you want to be annoyed — while you *should* be annoyed — you can't help but marvel at her endurance. Penny is the cockroach of office life: chaotic, indestructible, and weirdly thriving in an environment no one else could handle.

So laugh. Laugh when she pulls another mystery pill from her desk drawer. Laugh when she calls you from five yards away because she can't stand up. Laugh when she belts out *Total Eclipse of the Heart* into her shoe and still shows up Monday morning claiming she's "back on track."

Because Penny may be a mess. She may drain your patience. She may test the limits of human sympathy. But she'll also give you the best office stories you'll ever tell.

Because clowns can juggle, sure. But only Penny can juggle heartbreak, pharmaceuticals, and tequila — and somehow still keep her job.

Chapter Seven
The Inappropriate Dresser

THE INAPPROPRIATE DRESSER

Every workplace has a dress code. It might be "business casual." It might be "professional attire." Hell, it might just be "please wear pants." But wherever there are rules, there are people determined to break them — spectacularly.

Enter **The Inappropriate Dressers**: the coworkers who treat the office like their personal stage. They're not here to blend in. They're here to blindside you — and HR — with fashion choices so baffling, so distracting, so aggressively *them* that you'll spend meetings wondering if you've accidentally walked into a Vegas revue or a Comic-Con panel.

Vegas Vicki

Vicki doesn't do "subtle." She doesn't do "professional." What she does is **Vegas, baby.** Stilettos, plunging tops and skirts so short they're basically punctuation. HR has had "quiet words" with her more times than anyone can count, but she hears those words as compliments.

She's over 50, but still dresses like she's one wristband away from bottle service. She calls it "office attire." HR calls it "a liability." We call it "Tuesday."

Her outfits are so audacious they deserve their own Netflix documentary. There was the mini leopard-print skirt. The sequined halter top. The dress that could only be described as "made entirely of holes."

But her most legendary moment? The day she showed up in what can only be described as a **man's business shirt, cinched with a belt, and topped off with skyscraper heels.** No skirt. No trousers. Just one oversized shirt masquerading as "professional attire."

HR nearly fainted. The rest of us sat there wondering if we should call security or GQ. Vicki, of course, strutted through the office like she'd just invented fashion, oblivious to the fact that she looked less like a senior administrator and more like she was starring in a perfume ad called *Bad Decisions by Calvin Klein.*

But her defining moment, the day she dropped a pen mid-presentation, bent over to retrieve it, and the entire office learned her favorite underwear brand starts with a G. That was the day the quarterly forecast wasn't the only thing exposed.

Corporate Cosplay Carl

Carl, on the other hand, doesn't dress like he's heading to Vegas. Carl dresses like he's heading into battle... or maybe a LAN party.

Every morning is a new side quest. Monday? A Minecraft T-shirt stretched over a chest that's never seen a dumbbell. Tuesday? Mortal Kombat boots stomping down the hallway like he's about to finish someone. Wednesday? A trench coat so dramatic the interns whispered he was going to summon lightning during the staff meeting.

Carl doesn't just wear clothes — he builds characters. And he's so committed he once asked the entire office to call him *Skeletor*, his online gaming name. Management shut that down. The interns didn't. To this day, half the team still snickers, *"Morning, Skeletor,"* when he lumbers past the copier.

His crowning moment? Showing up to a team-building retreat with a full replica sword strapped to his back. *"Because a true warrior is never unarmed,"* he said. Nobody argued. Mostly because, again, sword.

The Classic Moves of the Inappropriate Dressers

You can't miss them. You don't want to see them. And yet, every Monday through Friday, they arrive — walking HR violations in heels and combat boots.

Vegas Vicki's Greatest Hits
The Shirt-That-Wasn't
The day she rocked up in a man's business shirt, cinched with a belt, paired with heels, and *nothing else*. She called it "chic." The rest of us called it "grounds for a lawsuit."

The G-String Reveal
The infamous presentation pen-drop, where she bent over and half the office discovered her favorite underwear brand. Productivity never recovered.

The Cougar Chic
Animal print everything. Leopard, zebra, snakeskin. It looked less like office attire and more like she rolled straight out of a zoo gift shop.

The Vegas Pool Party Look
Sequin halter top, short skirt, martini-at-11am energy. She didn't just break the dress code — she danced on its grave in six-inch stilettos.

The "Business Casual" Misunderstanding
Vicki heard "casual" and thought it meant "lingerie with a blazer." HR scheduled another "chat." She showed up in fishnets.

Corporate Cosplay Carl's Wardrobe Crimes

The Minecraft Monday
A stretched-out pixelated tee paired with cargo pants that hadn't seen detergent since the Obama administration. He called it "retro." We called it "tragic."

The Mortal Kombat Boots
Heavy leather stompers better suited for a nightclub bouncer than a budget analyst. Every step echoed through the office like he was declaring war on the carpet.

The Trench Coat Wednesday
Floor-length black trench coat in the middle of summer. He said it was "part of the vibe." The interns whispered he was going to summon lightning during the staff meeting.

The Skeletor Rebrand
The week he asked everyone to call him *Skeletor*, his gaming handle. HR said no. The interns said yes. To this day, the nickname sticks harder than his cologne.

The Sword Incident
The crown jewel: showing up to a team-building retreat with a full replica sword strapped to his back. *"A true warrior is never unarmed,"* he declared. Nobody disagreed — mostly because he had the sword.

Together, they're less "business casual" and more "unpaid extras in two different movies." She's *Vegas After Dark*, he's *Comic-Con Side Quest*, and both of them somehow ended up in your budget meeting.

The Toll on Your Sanity

Working with the Inappropriate Dressers isn't just distracting. It's psychological warfare. You sit at your desk, trying to focus on quarterly projections, and suddenly you're confronted with Vicki strutting past in six-inch stilettos or Carl clomping around in Mortal Kombat boots.

It's not just bad taste. It's a full-scale assault on your will to live.

The Eye Contact Problem
You can't look at them. You *try* to look at them — politely, professionally — but your eyeballs betray you. They wander to the sequins. They dart to the trench coat. And suddenly you're trapped in a staring contest with Vicki's neckline or Carl's foam Minecraft sword. HR says, *"Maintain professionalism."* But how?

How do you type up a report while Skeletor is asking if you've "leveled up" your Excel skills?

The Meeting Disaster

Imagine trying to concentrate during a quarterly budget review while Vicki's blouse is hanging on for dear life, or Carl is doodling Dungeons & Dragons maps in his notepad. Everyone pretends not to notice, but they notice. And once you've noticed, you can't unsee it. The meeting's over. Productivity's dead.

The Client Horror

It's one thing when they humiliate themselves internally. It's another when clients get involved. Remember the day Carl showed up to a pitch in combat boots and fingerless gloves? Or when Vicki wore a sequined mini-dress to the annual shareholder meeting? Clients don't forget. They go back to their offices and tell *their* coworkers about "the freak show" down the street. And suddenly, your company has a reputation.

The HR Fatigue

You'd think HR would put an end to it. But no. HR is tired. HR has given up. HR has had "a word" so many times that they now just close the blinds, sigh, and pretend sequins are in the policy handbook.

The Colleague Collateral Damage

It's not just you. It's everyone. Vicki distracts the interns. Carl terrifies the accountants. Nobody's immune. Every time they walk through the office, heads swivel like it's a tennis match nobody wanted to attend. You don't *work* with them. You *survive* them.

Working alongside the Inappropriate Dressers isn't just a job. It's a test of endurance. A slow, grinding sanity check. And the longer you last, the more you start to wonder maybe it's not them.

Maybe it's *you*. Maybe you're the crazy one for expecting normal clothes in a professional workplace.

Spoiler: you're not.

They're lunatics. And you're stuck watching the fashion show from hell.

Survival Guide: How to Endure the Inappropriate Dressers

Survival Guide: How to Endure the Inappropriate Dressers

When you're forced to share oxygen with Vegas Vicki and Corporate Cosplay Carl, you need more than patience. You need a survival strategy. Here's the extended playbook — equal parts practical advice, emergency measures, and spiritual coping mechanisms.

Step 1: Protect the Eyes

Forget screen strain — the real danger to your vision is Vicki's outfits. One wrong glance and you're blinded by sequins, exposed to more leg than a Vegas cabaret, or accidentally making eye contact with a neckline that plunges into the Mariana Trench.

Invest in tinted glasses. Pretend you're "sensitive to light." Really, you're sensitive to Vicki.

Carl's not any better. His trench coats and leather boots radiate "comic-con dad energy" that sucks you in against your will. Without protection, you'll start asking questions like, *"Is Skeletor a management position?"*

Step 2: Build Furniture Fortresses

Plants. Filing cabinets. Whiteboards. Anything you can use to create a barrier between their outfits and your sanity. Think of it as corporate feng shui, except instead of balancing chi, you're blocking sequins and replica swords.

One colleague once wheeled a whiteboard into place just to survive an entire week of Carl's Mortal Kombat boots. HR thought it was "strategic brainstorming space." Really, it was a barricade against trauma.

Step 3: Master the Zoom Half-Truth

If they're assigned to your project, suggest video calls "for convenience." The beauty of Zoom is you only see them from the waist up. Sure, Vicki's blouse might still defy physics, but at least you're spared the full-length fashion crimes. And Carl? Well, he's 90% trousers-as-costume. Crop the view, cut the damage.

Pro tip: never ask Carl to "stand and share." He will. And he'll be wearing chainmail.

Step 4: Emergency Deflection

When their outfits inevitably become the elephant in the room, learn to redirect attention like a magician.

Vicki struts past in nothing but a belted men's shirt? Immediately point out the weather. *"Hot day today, huh?"* Suddenly everyone's staring at the thermostat instead of her thighs.

Carl rolls in with a foam battle-axe? Ask about the quarterly figures. No one cares about numbers, but they'll pretend to just to avoid the cosplay carnage.

Step 5: The Client Damage-Control Kit

If external clients are involved, you need a pre-packed kit:

Neutral blazer (large enough to loan to Vicki in emergencies).

Spare tie (to throw at Carl when he shows up dressed like a wizard).

A printed "apologies for the attire" script you can casually slide across the conference table.

One colleague once whispered, *"She doesn't usually dress like this,"* during a client meeting while Vicki twirled in a sequined skirt. The client didn't believe it for a second.

Step 6: The HR Boomerang

Here's the thing: HR knows. They've known for years. But Vicki and Carl are unkillable. They've sat through so many "wardrobe consultations" they treat them like spa appointments.

So when HR dares to question *your* professionalism, play the nuclear card. Casually drop: *"Interesting. Should I bring up Carl's sword in the conference room? Or Vicki's shirt-as-dress era?"* Suddenly, HR backpedals so fast you hear tire squeals.

Step 7: Accept the Inevitability

At the end of the day, you can't fix them. You can't outlast them. They are eternal. Vicki will still be wearing sequins at 70. Carl will still be Skeletor long after you've quit. Your only real option is to turn their chaos into entertainment.

Laugh. Document. Share stories at the pub. Hell, write an entire chapter about them in a book called *Coworkers and Other Clowns*.

Because that's the only real survival strategy: embrace the madness.

Why Justice Never Comes

Here's the maddening truth: Vegas Vicki and Corporate Cosplay Carl should have been stopped years ago. The rules are clear, the complaints are whispered loudly enough, and the trauma is well-documented. Yet every Monday morning, there they are: sequins shimmering under the fluorescents, combat boots stomping past Accounts Payable.

Why? Because the system doesn't punish them. It protects them.

HR Fatigue

HR has sat them down so many times the words have lost meaning. "Professional attire." "Business standards." "Dress code expectations." It's white noise now. Vicki hears it as compliments. Carl hears it as "keep building your character arc." Eventually, HR just... gives up. They close the blinds, pretend leggings *are* trousers, and call it a day.

The "Performance Shield"

The cruel irony? They're often *good* at their jobs — or at least good enough to get away with murder-by-outfit. Vicki might terrify the interns, but she closes sales. Carl may look like a Mortal Kombat extra, but he can fix a spreadsheet faster than IT. And as long as they deliver *something*, management turns a blind eye to the fashion crimes.

The Office Legend Factor

They're no longer just employees. They're folklore. Vicki's G-string reveal? Still whispered about three years later. Carl's replica sword at the team retreat? Immortalized in memes on the office Slack. The longer they survive, the more untouchable they become. You don't fire legends — you suffer them.

The Client Shrug

Sure, clients notice. Of course they do. They walk out of meetings with stories they'll dine out on for months. *"You won't believe what she wore." "You won't believe what he called himself."* But as long as the invoices are paid and the work gets done, clients shrug it off. They'll laugh, they'll gossip, but they won't walk away.

The Nuclear Option Nobody Wants

Here's the real kicker: nobody *actually* wants to be the one to end them. Imagine being the poor manager who has to explain, in writing, that the reason Carl was terminated was "persistent cosplay." Or that Vicki was dismissed for "wardrobe choices resembling lingerie." Nobody wants to draft that paperwork. So everyone just lets it ride.

And so justice never comes. Vicki will keep strutting, Carl will keep cosplaying, HR will keep sighing, and you'll keep suffering. Because in the twisted hierarchy of office life, sequins and Skeletor always win.

Final Roast

Here's the thing about Vicki and Carl: they think they're icons. She struts in like she's auditioning for *Real Housewives of Accounts Payable*. He lumbers past like he's on his way to defend Castle Grayskull. They live for the attention, the whispers, the slack-jawed stares.

But everyone else? We're not inspired. We're exhausted.

Because when you show up to work, you expect fluorescent lighting, awkward small talk, maybe a stale muffin in the break room. You don't expect to be hit with Vicki's "shirt-as-a-dress" experiment or Carl's trench-coat-and-sword combo. You don't expect your professional career to feel like a crossover episode between *Vegas After Dark* and *Comic-Con: The Office Edition*.

And yet, somehow, they always survive. HR folds. Clients laugh. Management shrugs. The inappropriate dressers march on, immortal, untouchable, unrepentant.

So laugh. Laugh when Vicki claims sequins are "neutrals." Laugh when Carl insists on being called Skeletor. Laugh when they both somehow dodge another HR memo like it's a Nerf dart.

Because here's the truth: they'll never change. They'll still be here in ten years — Vicki tottering in leopard print, Carl clanking in cosplay boots. The only thing you can do is outlast them... and pray your next job has a stricter dress code.

Because clowns can juggle, sure. But they should never be in charge of a wardrobe.

Chapter Eight
The Meeting Hog

Some people build things, some people solve things — the Meeting Hog just books things. They don't just attend meetings — they *breed* them, multiplying calendar invites like rabbits on Red Bull. If there's a free slot in your week, they'll find it, fill it, and slap a vague subject line like *"Touch Base / Sync Up / Quick Chat."*

And here's the kicker: nothing — absolutely nothing — gets accomplished. You walk in hopeful, armed with a notepad. You walk out dazed, two hours older, and with less clarity than you started. Your only takeaway is the haunting realization that you'll never get those minutes back.

THE MEETING HOG

The Meeting Hog doesn't measure their worth in results. They measure it in airtime. They live for the sound of their own voice bouncing off conference room walls. They believe every story, tangent, and irrelevant anecdote is vital "context." Spoiler: it isn't.

But try escaping? Impossible. The moment you reach for your laptop, they hit you with: *"Just before you go..."* And suddenly you're chained to another 20 minutes of nonsense about printer toner budgets or their "big-picture vision" for stapler distribution.

The Meeting Hog isn't just wasting time. They're stealing lives. Yours, mine, and everyone who's ever dared to click "Accept" on their calendar invites.

The Classic Moves of the Meeting Hog

Recaps the Recap

Just when you think the torture's over, the Meeting Hog leans in with: *"Let's quickly summarize what we've covered..."* Then they proceed to repeat — in excruciating detail — every irrelevant tangent they started in the first place. Congratulations: you're now stuck in a Möbius strip of meeting hell.

Hijacks the Agenda

The calendar invite said *"Budget Review."* But ten minutes in, the Meeting Hog is telling a story about their nephew's soccer game, and somehow this detour ends with a debate on the ethics of office fridge cleaning. Nothing on the agenda is ever touched. Everything on your sanity is.

The 'One Last Thing' Gambit

The meeting is wrapping up. People are closing laptops. Someone even stands to leave. Then it happens: *"Oh, one last thing..."* Cue another 25 minutes of rambling about something that could have been an email. By the time they finish, your soul has left your body and joined the Wi-Fi router.

The Question Nobody Asked

Right as the meeting should end, the Hog raises their hand to ask the most irrelevant question imaginable. *"Have we considered how this aligns with our five-year vision?"* Five-year vision? Brenda, we're just trying to order new toner.

Tech Trouble Showboat

Every call, they forget how mute works. Every screen share, they can't find the button. Every time, they turn a five-second hiccup into a five-minute spectacle. "Can you hear me now? ...Now? ...Now?" Yes, Carl. We hear you. And we wish we didn't.

The Storyteller

Nobody asked, but the Meeting Hog insists on launching into *"a quick story"* that has nothing to do with the meeting. Suddenly, you know more about their vacation rental in Orlando than you do about the project deadline you're about to miss.

The Echo Chamber

They repeat everything someone else said — just louder and slower. You: *"We should test this on a smaller group first."* Them: *"Yes, what we REALLY need is a pilot program to validate results."* Everyone nods. You plot their demise.

The Toll on Your Sanity

Sitting through a Meeting Hog session isn't work. It's captivity. Time doesn't just move slowly; it folds in on itself. You start the meeting at 10:00 a.m., glance at the clock, and somehow it's still 10:07 — only now you've aged three years and your coffee is cold. They don't just waste minutes. They siphon hope. You walk in optimistic, thinking, *Maybe this time we'll be efficient.* Fifteen minutes later, you're staring at the table grain, fantasizing about spontaneous combustion. By the thirty-minute mark, you're Googling "how to fake a medical emergency convincingly." By the hour mark, you're considering career change: goat farming, treasure hunting, anything that doesn't involve Carl's "one last thought."

The psychological warfare is real. Every time someone tries to wrap up, the Hog interrupts. *"Just quickly..."* they begin — two words that never mean "quick." Those words are code for "buckle up, we're here until the janitor turns the lights off."

Your brain rebels. You start doodling in the margins of your notebook — first geometric shapes, then elaborate escape routes, then murder weapons. You mentally rehearse excuses you'll use next time: "Wi-Fi issues," "root canal," "urgent meeting with the Pope." None of them feel dramatic enough to escape.

The Hog doesn't just eat up hours — they make you question the meaning of life. You could have been working. You could have been resting. You could have been literally anywhere else. Instead, you're trapped, listening to someone explain synergy in four different accents.

And when it finally ends? Relief doesn't come. Because you know — deep down — that the calendar invite for *"Follow-Up Discussion"* is already waiting in your inbox.

Survival Guide: How to Outlast the Meeting Hog

Let's face it: you can't eliminate a Meeting Hog. They're not mortal. They feed on attention, inflate with calendar invites, and regenerate through "follow-up syncs." But you can *survive* them. Here's how:

The Step-Out Special
Keep a full water bottle at all times. When the Hog hits minute 42 of their tangent about toner, stand, whisper *"Sorry, refill,"* and leave. Never return. If questioned later, shrug and say *"hydration is important."* Nobody can argue with science.

The Frozen Screen Trick (Virtual Only)
On Zoom or Teams, tilt your head, stare blankly, and freeze like your Wi-Fi just died. Turn your camera off. Stay gone until the Hog has burned through their lungs. Come back with: *"Sorry, tech issues."* Everyone will envy your courage.

Weaponize Snacks
Crunchiest food possible: chips, carrots, celery. Every time the Hog starts a fresh tangent, take a bite. The louder the crunch, the shorter their story. It's Pavlovian training — and cathartic.

The Agenda Anchor
Print the agenda, hold it like a sacred scroll, and dramatically tap it every time the Hog strays off-topic. Bonus points for sighing audibly and muttering *"we're already 40 minutes behind."* Eventually, someone else will applaud you.

The Strategic Cough Attack
Fake a coughing fit when the Hog ramps up. If you do it well enough, you'll either get excused from the meeting or buy enough

chaos for someone else to cut them off. Warning: overuse may earn you a wellness check from HR.

Secret Side Hustle

Bring another project to work on: invoices, spreadsheets, your novel, a coloring book. While the Hog monologues about synergy, you'll at least walk out with progress on something that matters. Survival = productivity in disguise.

The Buddy System

Team up with a coworker. Develop signals: a raised eyebrow means "fake an emergency." A cough means "jump in and cut them off." Together, you can tag-team the Hog into silence. Like pro wrestlers, but sadder.

Calendar Judo

When the Hog sends an invite, counter with your own — same time, different subject, labeled *"Mandatory."* Half the office will pick yours. Divide and conquer.

The Escape Hatch

Keep one outrageous excuse in your back pocket. *"I'm so sorry, my neighbor's llama is loose again."* No one will question it. They'll just be grateful you left.

The Mental Vacation

When all else fails, leave your body. Daydream. Imagine life as a lighthouse keeper. Picture yourself winning the lottery. Pretend you're scuba diving with dolphins. Anything is better than listening to Brenda "circle back" for the twelfth time.

Bonus Activity: Meeting Hog Bingo

Print this out, tuck it under your notepad, and tick the boxes as the Hog eats your soul one tangent at a time. First to five earns the right to fake a bathroom emergency and never come back.

Says "circle back" more than three times in one meeting
Brings up a topic that has *nothing* to do with the agenda
"One last thing..." (adds another 25 minutes)
Asks a question that was already answered
Hijacks someone else's point and repeats it louder
Recaps the recap (you die a little inside)
Screen-share disaster — 10 minutes of "Can you see this?"
Tells a personal story no one needed
Makes a dad joke, then laughs at their own joke
Schedules a follow-up meeting before this one is even over
Uses a buzzword they don't understand (synergy, paradigm, alignment)
Talks through lunch, proudly oblivious to the growling stomachs

BINGO! You win... nothing. Except maybe a stronger case for remote work.

Why Justice Never Comes

Here's the injustice of it all: Meeting Hogs never get punished. Not once. Not ever.

The Boss Loves Them

For reasons no sane human can explain, bosses lap it up. They mistake rambling for leadership, jargon for vision, and sheer volume for confidence. The Hog says *"synergy"* loud enough and suddenly they're earmarked for promotion.

The HR Mirage

You dream of HR swooping in, clipboard in hand, ready to slay the Hog. It never happens. HR is too busy fighting bigger fires — like Vegas Vicki's wardrobe or Carl's sword. In comparison, the Hog is just "passionate."

The Office Stockholm Syndrome

Colleagues eventually stop complaining. They've been broken down, conditioned. After years of suffering, they start saying things like, *"Well, at least it keeps us from working,"* or, *"He means well."* This isn't acceptance. It's trauma bonding.

The Promotion Paradox

Here's the kicker: Hogs don't just survive, they *thrive*. They climb ladders powered entirely by hot air. They get promoted precisely because they never shut up. While you're quietly doing actual work, they're loudly taking credit for "shaping conversations."

That's why justice never comes. The system doesn't punish Hogs — it rewards them.

Final Roast

Here's the truth: the Meeting Hog will never stop. They'll never change. They'll never realize that nobody cares about their Bali trip, their PowerPoint slides, or their detailed analysis of printer toner economics.

Because to them, meetings aren't about progress. They're about performance. The Meeting Hog doesn't see a conference room — they see a stage. The rest of you aren't colleagues, you're their unpaid studio audience. Your groans are their laugh track. Your sighs are their applause.

And the cruelest joke of all? They think they're inspiring. They believe people leave the room enlightened, buzzing with their wisdom, whispering: *"Wow, Brenda really changed the game with that synergy slide."*

But really? The only things anyone leaves with are:

a migraine,

a stiff neck,

a doodle of a guillotine in their notebook,

and the quiet hope that lightning strikes the conference room next time — preferably right as the Hog says, *"One last point..."*

The Meeting Hog doesn't advance the company. They don't spark innovation. They don't solve problems. What they do is weaponize air. They inhale oxygen, exhale nonsense, and call it leadership.

They're not a thought leader. They're not a visionary. They're not even useful. They're the corporate version of a karaoke singer who refuses to give up the mic. They're not Whitney Houston, they're Gary from Accounting, slurring his way through *I Will Always Love You* for the fifth time while everyone begs for mercy.

And the worst part? They'll outlast you. You'll quit, transfer, or fake your own death, but the Meeting Hog will still be there, holding court, boring fresh recruits into early retirement. They are immortal. They are eternal. They are the unkillable cockroach of corporate life — except cockroaches at least know when to shut up.

So laugh. Laugh as they hijack another agenda. Laugh as they confuse airtime with brilliance. Laugh because you know the truth:

They're not the star of the show. They're not running the circus.

They're just a clown with a captive audience.

And the circus goes on.

Chapter Nine
Half-Day Stella

HALF-DAY STELLA

Every office has a Stella. She breezes in at 9:15 with a designer coffee and a glare that could curdle milk. She stays just long enough to terrorize the staff, drain morale, and remind everyone how "hopeless" they are — then vanishes by noon, like a storm cloud that only ruins mornings.

Stella doesn't work full days. She doesn't even work half days. She works *performance hours.* Her job isn't to do the work — it's to strut in, sigh loudly, criticize everything, and exit dramatically before lunch, leaving the rest of you to clean up both her mess and her spilled latte.

Her entire management style can be summarized in three steps: Arrive late, coffee in hand.

Deliver withering insults.

Disappear before HR can find her.

Stella isn't just lazy. She's strategically lazy. She's perfected the art of doing the absolute minimum while making everyone else feel like failures. And somehow — *somehow* — she still keeps her job.

Because here's the truth: Half-Day Stella knows something. She's got dirt on someone upstairs. She has *receipts*. She's bulletproof. And she weaponizes that immunity with the precision of a Bond villain.

And yes, one day, she spilled her coffee, slipped in it, and hit the floor like a sack of potatoes. Nobody helped. Not one person. We all left the room to laugh. Cruel? Maybe. Fair? Absolutely.

Classic Moves of Half-Day Stella

The Late Entrance (with Attitude)

She doesn't just arrive late — she *arrives late with fanfare*. Swooping into the office at 9:20, latte in hand, sunglasses still on, like she's Beyoncé entering a stadium. Except Beyoncé works harder in one soundcheck than Stella does all week.

The Coffee Critic

She'll take one sip, grimace dramatically, and complain about how "no one makes coffee right anymore." She's never made one herself. Not once. But apparently she's the Gordon Ramsay of office lattes.

The Drive-By Criticism

Her specialty: breezing past your desk, dropping a withering insult, and vanishing before you can respond. *"Is that the best you can do?"* she sneers, then disappears into her office like Batman if Batman was powered by spite instead of justice.

The Three-Hour Day
Her "workday" goes like this:
   9:15 — Arrive late.
   9:20 — Criticize everyone.
   9:45 — Loud phone call pretending to be important.
   10:30 — "Quick coffee catch-up" that lasts an hour.
   11:30 — Pack up.
   12:00 — Gone. Like smoke.

The HR Houdini
Somehow, HR never touches her. She's had more complaints than the company Wi-Fi, but she's still here. Why? Because Stella knows where the bodies are buried — or at least where the boss's expense receipts are.

The Coffee Spill Incident
The day karma struck. She spilled her own coffee, slipped in it, and crashed to the floor in a slow-motion symphony of schadenfreude. Nobody helped. Not one hand extended. The entire office silently filed out and laughed in the hall. Cruel? Maybe. Delicious? Absolutely.

The Exit Stage Left
By noon, she's out the door with a breezy, *"Don't stay too late, team!"* As if she hasn't just left you holding the flaming dumpster fire of her responsibilities.

The Comeback Queen
And yet — despite doing nothing, producing nothing, and contributing less than the office Ficus — Stella always comes back

the next day, smug as ever, ready to repeat the cycle. Because evil, apparently, never sleeps.

The Toll on Your Sanity

Working under Stella isn't just irritating — it's psychological warfare. You don't just lose patience. You lose faith in humanity.

The Morale Erosion

Imagine dragging yourself into the office early, coffee in hand, ready to grind. Stella strolls in an hour later, declares the team "hopeless," and leaves before lunch. By noon, she's gone, and you're left wondering why you bother trying.

The Stella Hangover

She's only physically present for three hours, but her impact lingers all day. It's like a bad perfume that clings to the office carpet. Every sigh, every eyeroll, every *"you'll never get this right"* echoes through your head long after she's fled the building.

The Team Bonding Through Hate

On the bright side, nothing unites coworkers quite like shared hatred. Stella is the office's common enemy — the final boss everyone secretly trains to defeat. People from different departments who never spoke before suddenly become allies, whispering in break rooms: *"She gone yet?"* *"Yup. Pub at five?"*

The Productivity Paradox

Ironically, Stella's absence makes the team more productive. Once she's out the door, shoulders relax, people breathe, and work actually gets done. The cruelest truth? The office runs smoother when its "manager" is already halfway to her afternoon gin and tonic.

The Karma Payoff

But nothing compares to the day Stella slipped on her own coffee. The sound of her heels skidding, the crash, the papers flying — it was workplace justice in surround sound. The silence that followed wasn't concern. It was awe. Then the entire office left the room to laugh. Cruel? Maybe. Cathartic? Oh, absolutely.

Working under Stella teaches you one thing: survival. You learn to endure insults, ignore hypocrisy, and find joy in her spectacular failures. Because if you don't laugh, you'll cry.

Survival Guide: How to Endure Half-Day Stella

The Morning Countdown

Don't think of her as a boss. Think of her as a storm system. She'll blow in at 9:15, wreak havoc for three hours, and be gone by lunch. All you need to do is bunker down until noon. Survive the first half of the day, and the afternoon is yours.

The Strategic Nods

When she dumps her daily insults, just nod. Don't argue, don't defend. Just nod like you're listening to a motivational speaker instead of the Wicked Witch of Accounts. This minimizes collateral damage and lets her move on to the next victim.

The Emergency Escape Plan

If she corners you with a "quick chat," activate your survival instincts: suddenly remember a dentist appointment, a fire drill, or that your car is double-parked. Doesn't matter if you don't own a car. Desperate times.

The Group Therapy Effect

Gather with your coworkers after she leaves. Mock her. Roast her. Bond over the absurdity. This is how you heal. Stella may break individuals, but she forges teams through mutual loathing.

The Calendar Trick

Schedule all important meetings for after lunch. Always. You don't want Stella swooping in with her coffee, derailing the agenda, and then disappearing before decisions get made. Afternoon is Stella-free — protect it at all costs.

The Laugh and Let Go

When she inevitably crashes — spilling her coffee, tripping over her own heels, or faking another "urgent client call" — laugh. Not in her face (unless you're quitting). But laugh. Because sometimes karma really does clock in on time, even if Stella never does.

Why Justice Never Comes

Here's the cruel truth: Half-Day Stella should've been gone years ago. But she's not. She's untouchable. And here's why:

The Dirt File

Stella knows things. She's got a mental filing cabinet of secrets — the boss's dodgy expenses, the director's "team-building" trip that looked suspiciously like a second honeymoon, the IT guy's side hustle selling printer ink on eBay. Fire her, and she'll burn the whole place down. Management knows it. That's why she stays.

The Optics Illusion

On paper, Stella looks... fine. Her timesheets don't show the three-hour days. Her reports (ghostwritten by you) make her look competent. Her bosses see her in meetings, hear her bark orders, and assume she's "taking charge." They never see her vanish by lunch.

The Fear Factor

Stella terrifies people. Not because she's powerful, but because she's petty. Anyone who crosses her gets buried under a mountain of passive-aggressive emails, calendar invites, and whispered gossip. It's easier to just let her clock out at noon than face her wrath.

The Office Legend Effect

Like it or not, Stella's a character. Her antics — the coffee slip, the dramatic sighs, the daily disappearing act — are part of office folklore. Firing her would be like cancelling the worst show on TV: sure, it's terrible, but everyone watches just to see what happens next.

And so, justice never comes. Stella stays. You suffer. The circus rolls on.

Final Roast

Half-Day Stella isn't a manager. She's a tourist. She pops in, ruins the scenery, and bails before the clean-up. She thinks she's the star of the show, but really she's the intermission act nobody paid to see. The warm-up comedian who bombs so badly the crowd just wants the headliner to start.

She'll never get fired. She'll never change. She'll keep breezing in at 9:15, sighing like she just discovered a new form of suffering, spilling her $7 oat latte, and vanishing by noon with a dramatic, *"Don't work too hard, team!"* as if the team hasn't been working *entirely in her absence* for years.

But here's the joke: Stella doesn't win, either. She'll never be respected, never be trusted, never be remembered for anything beyond being the office punchline. Her legacy is nothing more than the faded coffee ring she left on the boardroom table and the collective trauma she inflicted before lunch.

Nobody says, *"Remember Stella's leadership?"* They say, *"Remember when she slipped on her own coffee and HR had to call facilities to mop up the puddle of karmic justice?"* Nobody imitates her vision; they imitate her sigh, her glare, and her disappearing act.

Her résumé should just say:

Skills: arriving late, sighing loudly, leaving early.

Achievements: spilling coffee, dodging HR, perfecting the art of vanishing.

References: none, because everyone who worked with her hates her.

And yet, despite her three-hour reign of terror, Stella truly believes she's feared, respected, *essential*. She thinks she's holding the place together when really the office runs smoother the moment she's gone. Afternoons without Stella are like recess after detention — suddenly everyone can breathe again.

So laugh. Laugh at her latte wipeouts. Laugh at her smug little strut as she clocks out before noon. Laugh because the only thing shorter than her workday is her relevance. Laugh because she isn't a leader, she's a cautionary tale in heels.

Because Half-Day Stella isn't managing people. She's managing her Netflix queue. She's not steering the ship. She's the rat that sneaks on, chews through the snacks, and jumps overboard before the storm hits. She's not even a half-shift — she's a half-wit with a full sense of entitlement.

And when she's finally gone for good, her legacy won't be projects, policies, or promotions. It'll be the coffee stain, the faceplant, and the years of office folklore that start with the words: *"You won't believe what Stella did this time..."*

Because clowns can juggle, sure. But they can't survive a full shift. And Stella? She couldn't even make it to lunch.

Chapter Ten
Pass-the-Buck Pete

PASS-THE-BUCK PETE

Let's talk about Pete. The human Teflon. The man who's survived decades not by working hard, not by being smart, but by making sure every problem in his inbox lands in someone else's before 5 p.m.

Pete's not a leader. He's not even a worker. He's a middleman in khakis, a professional email forwarder, a human game of hot potato. His motto? *"If I can reply-all it, I don't have to solve it."*

He's lasted 40 years in corporate life, not by being good at his job, but by being **fantastically bad at accountability**. Deadlines missed? Not Pete's fault. Budget overspent? "Ask Finance."

Client unhappy? "Talk to Marketing." Fire in the server room? "IT should've prevented that." Pete could be standing in the middle of a burning office, holding a box of matches, and still manage to convince everyone it was Facilities' problem.

And somehow, this slippery little bureaucrat always walks out unscathed. While you're sweating bullets trying to fix the fallout, Pete's at his desk forwarding an email to you with the subject line: *"FYI – please action."*

The miracle isn't that Pete hasn't been fired. The miracle is that he's walking out of this mess with a fat pension and more superannuation than the people who actually carried him for decades.

Pete doesn't solve problems. Pete *exports* them. And he's made a career out of it.

Classic Moves of Pass-the-Buck Pete

The Inbox Hot Potato
Pete's entire workflow is built around one sacred ritual: forwarding. Client complaint? Forward it. IT issue? Forward it. Misdelivered pizza order? Forward it. By 5 p.m., Pete's inbox is empty, and yours is overflowing. He goes home bragging about how "productive" he's been.

The FYI Assassin
His signature move: slapping *"FYI – please action"* on an email without context, instructions, or even reading it. Like a corporate sniper, he fires off responsibility with one click, then disappears into the shadows of Outlook.

The Meeting Deflector
Ask Pete a question in a meeting and watch the magic happen:

"*Good point. Let's circle back with Finance on that.*" Translation: not my circus, not my monkeys. Pete has the reflexes of a ninja when it comes to dodging accountability.

The Credit Collector

Here's the kicker: if something he's "delegated" actually goes well, Pete suddenly reappears like, "*Great work team. I'm glad I pushed this through.*" Pushed? Pete, the only thing you've pushed in 20 years is the "Forward" button.

The Calendar Ninja

When real responsibility looms, Pete magically has a "conflict." Client call at 3? Sorry, he's double-booked with an "important strategy session." Dig deeper, and that session turns out to be Pete sitting at his desk scrolling the news.

The Blame Teleporter

Pete doesn't just dodge blame — he teleports it. A project blows up? Suddenly, it was Marketing's decision. IT's system. Finance's oversight. You. Anyone. Pete has never once been the cause of a problem, despite somehow being in the middle of all of them.

The Pension Sprint

And let's not forget his ultimate play: the slow-motion run toward retirement. Pete's been exporting problems so long he's practically clocked out mentally. He's got one eye on his superannuation, the other on the clock, and absolutely zero on the disaster he just dumped in your inbox.

Pass-the-Buck Pete doesn't just survive — he thrives. Because in corporate life, accountability is optional, but plausible deniability is priceless.

The Toll on Your Sanity

Working with Pete doesn't feel like teamwork. It feels like babysitting a 50-year-old child who's mastered the art of shrugging. He doesn't just fail to help — he actively makes your life harder by exporting his disasters to you like a courier of chaos.

The Inbox Avalanche

Your day starts with a clean slate. By 10 a.m., Pete has forwarded you five client complaints, three budget questions, and one email from IT with the subject line: *"Phishing Alert – Do Not Click."* Pete clicked it. Pete forwarded it. Now it's your problem.

The Meeting Mirage

You go into meetings thinking progress will be made. Instead, you watch Pete in action, batting questions away like he's playing corporate dodgeball. *"That's more of a Finance issue,"* he says, while Finance stares at him like they'd love to staple him to his chair.

The Blame Game

A deadline slips, a project collapses, a client storms off — somehow, Pete walks away squeaky clean. You're left standing there holding the bag, explaining to management why everything went sideways, while Pete is already halfway out the door for his "important lunch."

The Emotional Drain

It's not just extra work. It's the erosion of your will to live. Every time Pete's name pops into your inbox, your heart sinks. Not because he's angry. Not because he's demanding. But because you *know* he's just lobbed another problem over the fence.

The Pete Hangover

By the end of the day, you're exhausted. Not from your work, but from Pete's work. You've fixed his mistakes, soothed his clients, covered his missed deadlines. He's at home sipping wine, bragging to his spouse about how he "kept the team on track today." You're at your desk Googling "early retirement schemes" and "jobs that don't involve email."

Working with Pete is like cleaning up after a toddler who never grows up. Except toddlers are cute, and Pete is... Pete.

Survival Guide: How to Survive Pass-the-Buck Pete

The Inbox Firewall

Set up filters so every email Pete sends goes straight to a "Pete Problems" folder you'll never open. If it's truly urgent, someone else will scream about it eventually.

The Reply-All Trap

When Pete forwards you an issue, hit *Reply All* and tag three other departments. Suddenly, Pete's lost in the same mess he created. Watch him squirm as his own buck-passing gets passed right back to him.

The Fake Expert Gambit

Start replying with jargon so dense even Pete can't follow it. *"This requires a cross-functional workflow analysis leveraging predictive KPIs and upstream reconciliation."* Pete will nod, pretend to understand, and never bother you about it again.

The Meeting Grenade

When Pete tries to deflect in a meeting, throw the ball back hard: *"Actually Pete, you were closest to this issue — why don't you walk us through your approach?"* Sit back and enjoy as he panics like a deer in a PowerPoint.

The Deadline Boomerang

When Pete dumps a problem on you at 4:59 p.m., respond with: *"Got it, Pete — looping you back in for final sign-off by 9 a.m. tomorrow."* Congratulations: you've just returned the package to sender.

The Pete-Free Zone

Schedule important meetings at times Pete is guaranteed to be unavailable — like Friday afternoons, or literally any time there's free food in the cafeteria. It's the only way to get real work done.

The Nuclear Option

Forward one of Pete's emails back to him. With no edits. Just his own nonsense. Watch the confusion dawn as he realizes he's finally managed to pass the buck... back to himself.

With enough practice, you won't just survive Pete — you'll become immune to him. You'll read his "FYI – please action" with the same emotion you feel for spam mail. You'll recognize his tactics instantly and deflect them right back. And maybe, just maybe, you'll live long enough to see him retire — forwarding his problems to God Himself.

The Pete Bingo Card

Keep a secret bingo grid in your notebook. Mark a square every time Pete pulls one of his classics:

    "FYI – please action" with no context
Forwarded phishing scam

Mysterious "calendar conflict"
"Not my department" deflection
Takes credit for work he didn't touch
Sighs loudly while doing nothing
Vanishes before deadline
Sends an email back to the sender *he was supposed to answer*

Five in a row = you've won! Your prize? Another one of Pete's problems.

Why Justice Never Comes

Here's the gut punch: Pete doesn't just survive. He thrives. He's proof that corporate Darwinism doesn't reward the smartest, the hardest working, or the most innovative. No. It rewards the slipperiest. The least useful animals. The ones who know how to play dead until the predator leaves.

The Illusion of Busyness

Pete is a master illusionist. At first glance, he looks like a man buried in work — always typing, always clicking, always sighing dramatically as though juggling a million priorities. But watch closely, and you'll notice he's never actually *doing* anything.

That furious typing? He's forwarding spam to you with *"FYI – please action."*

That spreadsheet open on his screen? It's been frozen on the same tab for an hour.

That sigh? It's not workload. It's indigestion from his fourth muffin of the morning.

To upper management, it looks like hustle. To you, it looks like spam. Pete is a magician whose only trick is shoving the rabbit into someone else's hat.

The Scapegoat Shuffle

Pete never stands alone when disaster strikes. He's like a con artist with a deck of scapegoats. Something goes wrong? He deals out blame like playing cards:

"That was Marketing's decision."
"Finance dropped the ball."
"IT never flagged it."
"Operations should have caught it."

By the time you realize Pete was even involved, he's already vanished into the shadows, leaving someone else holding the smoking gun. It's not just passing the buck. It's passing the entire crime scene to another department.

The Corporate Camouflage

Pete is beige in human form. Beige ties. Beige personality. Beige results. He blends so seamlessly into the wallpaper of corporate life that nobody notices him. He's never brilliant enough to draw attention. Never bad enough to get fired. He's the middle lane of the highway — boring, steady, impossible to remove without disrupting traffic. And beige, as it turns out, is indestructible.

The Retirement Shield

The closer Pete gets to retirement, the safer he becomes. Management doesn't want to start a fight with someone who's already got one loafer out the door. Why bother? Better to let him coast into the sunset, dragging a pension bigger than the GDP of a small country. Pete knows it. He flaunts it. He wears his looming retirement like armor: untouchable, unbothered, unstoppable.

And that's why justice never comes. Pete is corporate Teflon — nothing sticks, nothing breaks, nothing changes. He's proof that if you do just enough to look alive, but never enough to take responsibility, the system won't just tolerate you. It'll reward you.

Final Roast

Pass-the-Buck Pete isn't a leader. He isn't even a worker. He's a courier service in khakis. He's spent forty years perfecting the ancient art of saying: *"Not my problem."*

His greatest skill isn't solving problems. It's exporting them. He's the human version of "redirected mail." The corporate Amazon driver who keeps leaving your packages at the wrong house. The man whose entire career could be summed up with one button: *Forward.*

Pete doesn't produce solutions. He produces confusion. He doesn't deliver results. He delivers headaches. If there were a corporate Olympics, Pete would medal in "Most Likely to Shift the Blame Before Lunch."

And yet, he'll walk out of this place rich. Decades of passing the buck, decades of dodging blame, decades of shoving responsibility into someone else's inbox — and Pete's reward is a fat pension, a gold watch, and a farewell cake he didn't even organize. (He'll probably make someone else cut and serve it, too.)

But here's the truth: nobody respects him. Nobody will remember him fondly. He won't be toasted at reunions or honored in newsletters. His name will live on only in the whispered curses of every coworker who ever opened an email labeled *"FYI – please action."*

Pete is not a mentor. He's not a role model. He's not even an example of what *to do*. He's a cautionary tale. Proof that mediocrity, when paired with slipperiness, can outlast brilliance. Proof that corporate life is less survival of the fittest and more survival of the slipperiest.

So laugh. Laugh at the hot potatoes, the dodges, the endless spam. Laugh at the way Pete could turn even a phishing scam into someone else's problem. Laugh because the only thing Pete ever produced was more work for everyone else.

And one day, when he finally walks out for good, the office won't cry. They won't miss him. They won't write heartfelt tributes. They'll cheer. Not because he's gone, but because for the first time in decades, the buck will finally stop.

Because clowns can juggle, sure. But Pete never even learned how to catch.

Chapter Eleven
Transient Supermodel

Mission in High Heels

The Transient Supermodel isn't here to climb the corporate ladder. She's not even here to hold it steady while someone else climbs. She's here for one thing, and one thing only: to find her ticket out of the office. And that ticket usually comes with a six-figure salary, a waterfront property, and a set of initials after his name.

She's not confused about life. She's not "finding herself." She's not "just seeing where this role takes her." Please. She knows exactly where she wants to go: straight into the passenger seat of a Porsche, preferably before her next birthday.

The office is just a hunting ground. A networking lounge. A live-action dating app with better lighting. Every smile is bait. Every laugh is strategy. Every wardrobe choice is military-grade husband-hunting gear. While the rest of us are struggling to finish PowerPoint decks, she's already plotting her next romantic ambush by the water cooler.

And here's what makes her truly terrifying: she's efficient. She's not wasting time. She's a woman on a mission, and her beauty is her weapon. She knows it has a shelf life, and she's cashing in before it expires. Ruthless? Yes. Admirable? Weirdly, also yes.

Classic Moves of the Transient Supermodel

The Catwalk Commute

She doesn't just walk into the office. She *arrives*. Heels clicking like a metronome of confidence, perfume drifting behind her in a chemical fog strong enough to trigger HR's air-quality policy. Sunglasses stay on until she's at her desk, as if the fluorescent lights are paparazzi flashes. You show up with a half-empty coffee and a bagel stain on your shirt; she arrives like she's shooting a fragrance ad.

And yes, it's ridiculous. But you also kind of envy it. Who wouldn't want to start every day as if the world was clapping just for them?

The Desk-as-Runway

Normal people sit in chairs. Not her. She perches on the edge of her desk like it's a magazine cover shoot. One leg crossed, phone angled for selfies, coffee cup staged like a prop. Her "workspace" is less about productivity and more about aesthetics — perfectly messy notebooks, curated stationery, and at least one vase of flowers that somehow never wilts.

It's impractical. It's absurd. It's also genius branding. While your desk screams *"overworked office drone,"* hers whispers *"aspirational lifestyle influencer."*

The Strategic Outfit

Every ensemble is calculated. Monday: the "approachable but intriguing" look for scoping out new hires. Wednesday: "slightly too much cleavage" in case there's an after-work networking event. Friday: "Vegas cocktail hour meets business casual," because HR's too tired to fight it before the weekend.

The skirts are short. The heels are tall. The tops are plunging enough to make the copy machine blush. It's outrageous — but strategic. Fashion is her sword and shield, and she wields it better than most people manage spreadsheets.

The Flirt & Flee

She's mastered the art of micro-flirtation. A hair flip, a quick giggle, a brush of the arm. Just enough to spark interest, never enough to seem committed. Then she's gone, drifting across the office before you've even processed what happened.

It's infuriating, but it's also a skill. Where you stumble through small talk and awkward pauses, she's perfected the two-minute power play.

The Lunch Hour Photoshoot

You eat your sad sandwich hunched at your desk. She spends her entire lunch break outside, posing with kale salads she won't eat. She snaps selfies, tweaks angles, and uploads captions like *#Work-*

Lunch #BossBabe #GlowUp.

It's cringe-worthy. But it's also clever. While you're chewing through soggy bread, she's marketing herself as a lifestyle brand.

The LinkedIn Illusionist

Her résumé is a work of fiction. "Brand Consultant," "Strategic Advisor," "Wellness Entrepreneur." Translation: she once handed out flyers, helped set up a tradeshow booth, and briefly sold protein shakes online.

But her LinkedIn profile? It's a masterpiece. High-quality headshots, buzzwords galore, and endorsements from people you've never heard of. It looks like she's run half the Fortune 500. And honestly? You kind of wish you had her audacity.

The Husband Hunt (Mission Mode)

Let's be clear: she's not here for a promotion. She's here for a proposal. The office is just her aquarium, and she's fishing for the richest guppy. Doctors, bankers, execs — all fair game. Every coffee break is reconnaissance, every after-work drink is a mission, every company retreat is a potential ambush.

Is it shameless? Absolutely. But at least she's decisive. While the rest of us waffle about "career goals," she's laser-focused on *life goals*.

The Dramatic Exit

She doesn't leave quietly. Ever. There's always an email with inspirational quotes, a desk cleared out in record time, or a suspiciously vague "pursuing new opportunities in wellness" announcement. Colleagues gossip for weeks. HR sighs. The office feels lighter — and messier — because she never actually finished her work.

But while you're stuck cleaning up her projects, she's already posting glamorous "new chapter" selfies with hashtags like *#Movin-*

gOn #Manifesting #Blessed. And the wild part? She always lands on her feet.

The Toll on Your Sanity

Working with the Transient Supermodel feels less like having a colleague and more like being cast as an unpaid extra in her never-ending reality show. Every meeting turns into background noise for her charisma performance. She's not taking notes — she's adjusting her hair in the reflection of her laptop screen. She's not contributing to the project plan — she's planning her outfit for drinks with "a friend" after work.

Clients notice her. Bosses protect her. Coworkers gossip about her. And meanwhile, you? You're stuck doing the work she leaves behind like a stagehand cleaning up glitter after a Vegas revue.

Your workload doubles because while you're typing reports and updating spreadsheets, she's busy taking selfies in the conference room under the "good lighting." She drops out of projects halfway through, leaving chaos in her wake, and somehow, the mess lands squarely on your desk. You'll be knee-deep in deadlines while she floats past chirping, *"Oh my God, you're amazing for picking that up, thank youuu!"*

The stress is relentless. She always has an "appointment." A vague "lunch." A mysterious "doctor's visit" that stretches for three hours and ends with her returning in a new outfit. And because she's hot, charismatic, and untouchable, management waves it off. *"She's got a lot on her plate right now,"* they say, as if Pilates class and Bumble dates count as deliverables.

Morale plummets because you know she'll get away with it — again. She's never punished, never called out, never made to face the mountain of work she leaves behind. You'll grind late into the night to keep the team afloat, and she'll glide out the door at 4 p.m. with a breezy, *"See you tomorrow!"*

And yet… you can't look away. She's infuriating, but she's hypnotic. She's a car crash in couture: terrible, disruptive, impossible to ignore. You hate the extra hours, the endless cleanup, the constant chaos. But a tiny part of you also admires the sheer audacity. She's not working harder — she's working smarter, in the most shameless way possible. And while you're exhausted, she's untouchable.

Because here's the brutal truth: the Transient Supermodel isn't just surviving the office. She's thriving in it, precisely because she refuses to play by the rules the rest of us are chained to. And while you admire her boldness, it means you're the one quietly holding the company together while she's holding auditions for her next rich husband.

Survival Guide

Don't Compete.

You will not win. She's armed with cheekbones sharp enough to cut glass and the kind of confidence that can't be taught. You could have a double MBA, a decade of experience, and a brilliant proposal — but the boss will still be too busy staring at her contouring to notice your spreadsheet. Accept it. Play your own game.

Stay Out of the Splash Zone.

When she exits (and she always exits), she leaves chaos in her wake. Projects half-finished. Emails unanswered. Client deliverables abandoned like orphaned puppies. The trick? Don't be the one standing nearest her desk when the storm hits. Because cleanup duty always falls to whoever makes eye contact with management first.

Document Everything.

Screenshots, email threads, timestamps — keep receipts like you're prepping for a custody battle. Because when she vanishes mid-project to "pursue new opportunities," someone's going to demand answers. With proof, you can at least prove it wasn't you. Without proof? Congratulations, you just inherited her workload.

Avoid the Lunch Trap.

She'll invite you to "grab a salad," and you'll think, *Finally! Maybe she's being normal.* Wrong. Lunch is never lunch. It's a content-creation session. You'll end up holding her phone while she poses with avocado toast at twenty different angles. You'll leave hungry, humiliated, and possibly tagged in a post captioned *#TeamLunch #WorkBesties,* even though she doesn't know your last name.

Invest in Noise-Cancelling Headphones.

Not for her voice. For the click-clack of her heels echoing like a metronome of superiority across the office floor. Also helpful for drowning out the perfume-induced sneezes of your colleagues.

Master the Deadpan.

When she flirts, don't feed the performance. Don't giggle. Don't fumble. Stare back with the blankest face possible until she drifts away to someone more responsive. It won't stop her — but it will buy you thirty seconds of peace.

Treat Her Like Entertainment.
The healthiest survival tactic is to stop pretending she's a coworker. She's not. She's office cabaret. She's there to dazzle, distract, and eventually disappear. You're not her colleague; you're her audience. So sit back, relax, and enjoy the free show.

Learn From Her Shamelessness.
And here's the kicker: maybe, just maybe, there's a lesson here. While you're burning out to prove your worth, she's leveraging hers with zero guilt. While you're terrified of being judged, she's immune. She knows exactly what she wants and isn't afraid to pursue it — loudly, unapologetically, and with sequins. You don't have to admire her, but you can steal a page from her playbook: sometimes confidence is worth more than competence.

Bingo Card

Inspirational LinkedIn post about "new opportunities"
  Vague "doctor's appointment" → outfit change
  "You're amazing, thank youuu!" after dumping work on you
  #Manifesting hashtag in farewell email
  #BossBabe selfie at lunch

Why Justice Never Comes

Here's the brutal truth: The Transient Supermodel doesn't just survive in corporate life — she thrives. And not because she's brilliant, innovative, or hardworking. No. She thrives because she knows the one secret everyone else is too scared to say out loud: in the workplace, competence is optional, but charisma is currency.

Bosses love her. They don't care that she hasn't opened Excel since the Bush administration. They care that she lights up the conference room, that clients smile when she floats in, that photos from company events suddenly look like magazine spreads. She's "good for morale," they say, mistaking her chaos for culture.

Clients adore her too. Never mind that she can't explain a single detail of the project — she leans forward, laughs at the right moment, and asks one "thoughtful" question that sounds deep but means nothing. *"How does this align with our vision?"* she'll chirp, and suddenly the client feels like they're in the presence of brilliance. Meanwhile, you're sweating through the actual work.

Even HR, the supposed guardians of professionalism, won't touch her. They know her outfits are inappropriate. They know her perfume is a workplace hazard. They know her LinkedIn updates are more fiction than fact. But they also know that calling her out risks a scene — and HR's worst nightmare isn't misconduct. It's drama.

And so she floats above it all, immune to consequences. She can leave projects half-finished, vanish for "appointments," skip deadlines, even openly flirt with management — and still, somehow, she's praised as "a valuable team player."

Why? Because she's not playing the same game. You're grinding for promotions, trying to prove your worth. She's fast-tracking to her next destination: a richer man, a bigger house, a shinier Instagram bio. You're climbing the corporate ladder rung by rung. She's base-jumping straight to the yacht.

Justice never comes for her because she doesn't need it. Justice is for people stuck playing by the rules. She's not. She's rewriting them.

And the rest of us? We're left doing double the work, muttering in the break room about fairness, while she's already halfway out the door in a new outfit, updating her followers with *#NewChapter #Manifesting.*

Final Roast

The Transient Supermodel isn't a coworker. She's a tourist. She breezes in, dazzles the locals, and vanishes when the free drinks run out. Her desk isn't a workstation; it's a runway. Her job title isn't "Marketing Coordinator" or "Admin Support." It's "Wife-in-Training."

She doesn't produce deliverables. She produces *content*. She doesn't finish reports. She finishes Instagram reels. She doesn't grind for promotions. She grinds through men with a six-figure salary cap. And the worst part? It works.

Her greatest skill isn't collaboration. It's reinvention. In six months, she can spin a half-assed stint in Accounts Payable into "Financial Strategist." She can turn answering phones into "Client Relationship Manager." And she can turn quitting via a dramatic email into a "career pivot into wellness." While you're sweating over bullet points on your résumé, she's already photoshopped herself into a corner office that never existed.

And yes, you'll hate her for it. You'll resent every unfinished project, every botched handover, every time you had to stay late because she vanished for an "appointment." You'll curse her name while buried under her workload.

But here's the kicker: you'll also remember her. Because she's not beige. She's not forgettable. She's not like the rest of us trudging through decades of office monotony. She's chaos in stilettos, audacity in lipstick, and ambition in the rawest, most shameless form.

She's not building a career. She's building a launchpad. She's not networking. She's hunting. She's not here for the pension plan. She's here for the *escape plan*. And she'll pull it off — because she always does.

So laugh. Laugh at the selfies, the outfits, the chaos. Laugh at the fact she did less work in a year than you did in a week and still got praised. Laugh because while you're the backbone of the office, she's the spectacle — and spectacle always wins.

Because clowns can juggle, sure. But the Transient Supermodel doesn't juggle at all — she struts, she poses, she flirts, she vanishes. And somehow, impossibly, she gets exactly what she came for.

And you? You're the one left holding the balls.

Chapter Twelve

The Retired-in-Spirit Guy

He's not retired yet — technically. HR still cuts him a paycheck, his email address still works, and his name still appears on the org chart. But make no mistake: this man checked out years ago. His body is at the desk, but his soul is already in a deckchair somewhere with a piña colada.

He's got two years to go, maybe less, and he's coasting so hard he's practically horizontal. Projects? Not his problem. Deadlines? Someone else's issue. Innovation? That's for the kids. He's just here to collect the last few paychecks before his pension kicks in and he vanishes into permanent leisure.

And he doesn't hide it. Oh no. If anything, he flaunts it. He'll stroll in late, settle into his chair with a sigh loud enough to shake the blinds, and announce, *"Two more years, folks. Then I'm free."* It's not a secret. It's his entire personality.

While you're scrambling to prove yourself, climb ladders, and survive quarterly reviews, he's leaning back, smirking, and saying things *like, none of this will matter when I'm fishing in Florida.* And honestly? He might be the most infuriating — and enviable — clown in the office.

Classic Moves of The Retired-in-Spirit Guy

The Countdown Clock
He doesn't just know how long he's got left — he announces it. Loudly. Constantly. *"Eighteen months, three weeks, and two days,"* he'll mutter like a prisoner scratching tallies into a cell wall. Except he's not trapped. He's just waiting for his pension to land.

The Shrug of Indifference
Deadlines? He shrugs. Targets? He shrugs. The building could be on fire and he'd still shrug, mumble *"not my problem soon,"* and walk out at his usual 3:45 p.m. For everyone else, it's work. For him, it's background noise on the way to freedom.

The Early Exit
His contract might say 9 to 5, but his spirit left at 2:30. By 3:00, he's packing up. By 3:15, his chair is spinning. By 3:30, he's in the parking lot, whistling like a man with zero consequences left to face.

The War Story
He'll interrupt any meeting with a long, meandering tale about

"how we did it back in '92." It's not helpful. It's not relevant. But it burns fifteen minutes, and wasting time is his greatest joy.

The Bare-Minimum Mastery

He doesn't say no. He doesn't say yes. He does *just enough* to avoid disciplinary action. A single email reply here. A single bullet point on a report there. He's like a magician who specializes in the disappearing act — except instead of applause, he gets paychecks.

The Bad Influence

You'll be grinding late into the night, and he'll stroll past your desk saying, *"Don't kill yourself over it, kid. They don't pay you enough."* And damn it, he's right. But instead of helping, he's just planting the seeds of apathy like corporate Johnny Appleseed.

The Retirement Brochure Enthusiast

While you're browsing work emails, he's browsing travel packages. His desk is covered in cruise flyers, real estate listings, and golf-course brochures. Every Zoom call background? A new tropical wallpaper. Subtle, he is not.

The Smug Untouchable

He's bulletproof. Everyone knows he's checked out, but nobody calls him on it. Why bother? In two years, he'll be gone, sailing into the sunset while you're still stuck covering his workload.

The Toll on Your Sanity

Working alongside the Retired-in-Spirit Guy is like sitting next to a living, breathing spoiler alert for your own career. He's not just coasting toward retirement — he's narrating your future in real time, and it's bleak.

Bright-eyed graduate walks in, full of ambition? He chuckles darkly. *"Give it twenty years, son. You'll be just like me. The fire goes out eventually."* Suddenly, that new starter pack of sticky notes feels like a death sentence.

You stay late, desperate to impress the boss? He passes by your desk, shakes his head, and mutters, *"Doesn't matter how hard you work. They'll still forget your name when you're gone."* Thanks, Gerry. That's the motivational poster we didn't need.

Every conversation with him drips with grim wisdom. He doesn't warn you against becoming him — he assures you it's inevitable. He's not a mentor. He's a museum exhibit: *"This is what you'll look like after forty years of corporate servitude. Please do not tap the glass."*

And the worst part? He's not wrong.

His cynicism seeps into the air-conditioning. It kills morale faster than budget cuts. While you're trying to psych yourself up for "opportunities," he's there to remind you that promotions don't fix anything, managers don't care, and that dream of making a difference? Hilarious.

The toll isn't just the extra work you inherit when he checks out of projects. It's the way he makes you question your own choices. *Am I wasting my life? Will I become him? Do I really want to give this place four decades only to shuffle out with a gold watch and arthritis?*

Working near him feels like working beside the Ghost of Career Future — and every sigh, shrug, and half-hearted email he sends is another nail in your motivational coffin.

Survival Guide

The Earplug Method
You can't stop him from telling you how miserable the job is, but you can limit how much of it reaches your brain. Invest in earbuds. Pretend you're on a call. Fake nods. Just don't let the words sink in, or you'll start updating your résumé by lunch.

The Deflection Game
He'll try to corner you with *"Don't bother working late — they'll forget you in five years."* Your only weapon is redirection. Smile, nod, and ask about his golf swing, his fishing plans, or which cruise brochure he's drooled on today. Keep him in retirement fantasy mode, not career-ruin prophecy mode.

The Workload Firewall
His favorite move is sliding unfinished projects onto your desk like a dealer tossing cards. The trick is learning how to say no without saying no. *"That's above my pay grade." "Let me loop in the manager."* Bounce it back like hot potato. Otherwise, you'll be running two careers while he's running out the clock.

Learn From His Laziness
He's not wrong about everything. Sometimes the smartest move is not killing yourself for a company that would replace you by Wednesday. His cynicism is corrosive, but buried inside is a survival lesson: pace yourself. You don't need to adopt his apathy wholesale — just learn not to bleed for people who don't care if you exist.

The Pity Clap
Every so often, throw him a bone. Laugh at his "two more years" jokes. Congratulate him on booking that cruise. It keeps him smug

and distracted, and that means less time spent dragging you down into his motivational graveyard.

Build Your Exit Plan

His greatest gift is perspective. He's showing you what unchecked career stagnation looks like. Use that as fuel. Don't wait until you're sixty-two and dead inside. Build your escape strategy now — whether it's a new career, a side hustle, or just the knowledge that you won't be him.

Because you can't fix him, he does not want to be fixed, he has it sorted. You can only protect yourself. He's not a coworker anymore. He's a sad man in khakis.

Bonus Activity: Retired-in-Spirit Bingo

Print this, keep it in your drawer, and tick boxes whenever he strikes. First to five wins the right to cry in the bathroom about your own future.

Print this, keep it in your drawer, and tick the boxes whenever he strikes. First to five wins the right to cry in the bathroom about your own future.

Announces his retirement countdown to the exact day (*"Eighteen months, three weeks, and two days, kid."*)
Leaves at 3:15 p.m. sharp, chair still spinning
Brings travel brochures to a staff meeting and spreads them out like evidence
Says, *"Don't bother — none of this matters"* during a crisis meeting
Forgets your name, calls you "kid," "champ," or "sport"
Brags about his pension mid-crisis meeting while everyone else is panicking

Shrugs at a deadline like it's a weather forecast (*"Eh, rain tomorrow too."*)

Mentions fishing, golf, or "the good life" at least twice a day

Wastes 15 minutes telling a story that starts with *"Back in '92..."*

Has a desktop wallpaper of a tropical beach or a golf course

Prints cruise brochures on the office printer (using company paper, of course)

Spends the first ten minutes of every Zoom call complaining about "this newfangled technology"

Quietly deletes himself from group projects without telling anyone

Refuses new training because *"I'll be gone before it matters."*

Shows up late with the same excuse: *"Traffic was bad, but who cares, right?"*

Reminds you that you'll end up just like him (*"It's not if, it's when."*)

Nods off in a meeting and pretends it was "deep thinking"

Brings up his vacation plans in every unrelated conversation (*"That's interesting, but when I'm in Spain next summer..."*)

Why Justice Never Comes

Here's the thing: everyone knows he's done. His boss knows. HR knows. You know. Hell, he knows, and he's not shy about reminding you. And yet... nothing happens. Nobody calls him into a meeting. Nobody threatens disciplinary action. Nobody even raises an eyebrow when he disappears for two-hour lunches or closes his laptop at 3:15 p.m.

Why? Because at this point, he's untouchable.

The Pension Shield

He's so close to retirement that it's not worth the paperwork. Managers think, *"Why rock the boat? Let him coast."* And so he does — right into the sunset with a payout bigger than the GDP of a small island nation.

The Institutional Memory Card

Every company has a few dinosaurs who know the weird legacy systems, the old client quirks, or the admin passwords nobody else can remember. That's his trump card. Sure, he hasn't produced a full report in a decade, but when the CEO asks, *"Who set up the 2004 filing system?"* he's the only one who knows. That scrap of knowledge is his shield against accountability.

The Sympathy Factor

Even the most hard-nosed manager can't bring themselves to discipline someone who's "almost done." They look at him and see their own future: tired, checked out, desperate for freedom. They're not punishing him — they're preemptively pardoning themselves.

The Beige Camouflage

He doesn't stand out enough to get fired, and he doesn't screw up badly enough to make headlines. He's beige. Bland. Forgettable. And beige never gets dragged into HR. Beige just lingers until it quietly retires.

The Scapegoat Shuffle

When things go wrong, nobody blames him — because everyone knows he's useless already. The buck skips right over his desk and lands on yours. He's not the scapegoat. He's the empty chair in the corner that problems just float past.

And so justice never comes. Not because he deserves protection. But because it's easier for the company to let him drift. Easier to let him become a motivational black hole, sucking the hope out of younger employees, than to admit they've let dead weight sit on payroll for a decade.

Justice never comes because justice would require effort. And effort, like him, left the building years ago.

Final Roast

The Retired-in-Spirit Guy isn't an employee anymore. He's a ghost in khakis. A cautionary tale propped up at a desk, here to remind everyone what happens if you give your entire life to a company: you end up waiting out the clock, bitter, smug, and one vacation brochure away from a breakdown.

He's not mentoring anyone. He's haunting them. Every sigh, every shrug, every *"two more years, kid"* speech is another nail in the coffin of your youthful optimism. He's the Ghost of Career Future, drifting through the cubicles, rattling his chains of apathy.

But here's the paradox: as much as you hate him, part of you envies him. Because he's free. Truly free. While you're breaking your back for deadlines that no one will remember, he's already mentally on a beach, cocktail in hand, laughing at the poor fools still grinding away.

He'll never be fired. He'll never be called out. He'll coast all the way to the finish line, pocket a gold watch, and vanish into a retirement so cushy it makes your 401(k) look like pocket change.

And when he goes, nobody will miss him. They'll cheer. They'll high-five. They'll breathe a collective sigh of relief. Not because they respected him — but because his countdown finally hit zero.

So laugh. Laugh at the travel brochures, the indifference, the constant reminders that you too will wither into corporate beige if you're not careful. Laugh, because clowns can juggle, sure — but this clown dropped every ball years ago and still somehow got rewarded for it.

And maybe — just maybe — let his cynicism light a fire under you. Because the only thing scarier than working with him is realizing you're on track to *become him*.

Chapter Thirteen
Over-Promoted Mystery Manager

OVER-PROMOTED MYSTERY MANAGER

Every company has one: the Over-Promoted Mystery Manager. The corporate unicorn. The riddle in a lanyard. The person whose very existence raises the eternal question: *How the hell did they get here?*

They have no skills. None. They can't run a meeting without the PowerPoint crashing. They can't answer a question without stuttering into three unrelated tangents. They don't understand the software, the strategy, or even the acronyms. And yet — somehow — they're in charge.

They're not just unqualified. They're aggressively unqualified. You could pick a random intern, spin them around in a chair, and they'd land facing someone more competent. But while the rest of us claw for recognition, Mystery Manager waltzed into the corner office like they found a cheat code.

How? Nobody knows. Maybe they're somebody's cousin. Maybe they were the only one sober at the Christmas party when the CEO needed a scapegoat. Maybe they sacrificed a goat under a full moon and HR hasn't stopped shaking since. Whatever the reason, they've defied Darwinism. They are the corporate cockroach — thriving in conditions that kill everyone else.

And worst of all? They're indestructible. Layoffs come and go, departments are gutted, but Mystery Manager? Safe as houses. They survive everything. Like glitter, like that weird smell in the office, like that one voicemail from your ex you can't delete — they endure.

They don't inspire respect. They don't inspire loyalty. What they inspire is rage, disbelief, and the occasional fantasy about faking your own death just to get out of another one of their "strategy sessions."

The Over-Promoted Mystery Manager isn't here to lead. They're here to remind us all that meritocracy is a lie and incompetence, when packaged correctly, is bulletproof.

Classic Moves of the Over-Promoted Mystery Manager

The Buzzword Barrage

They don't understand the project, but they sure as hell know how to say *"synergy," "innovation,"* and *"circle back."* Their entire career is built on weaponizing buzzwords until everyone's too confused to call them out.

The Delegation Olympics

Every task, no matter how small, gets bounced to someone else. Writing an email? Too "high level." Approving a budget? Better "loop in Finance." Mystery Manager's desk is a black hole where responsibilities enter and never return.

The Meeting Marathoner

They live for meetings. Not because they accomplish anything — but because meetings are their camouflage. If you're constantly in a meeting, nobody can prove you don't do actual work. They'll schedule a 3-hour "alignment session" on stapler usage just to look busy.

The Credit Collector

Any team win magically becomes their win. Finished the project? Mystery Manager beams at the CEO: *"I really drove the team on this one."* Meanwhile, you're still wiping blood, sweat, and tears off your keyboard.

The Blame Shifter

When things go wrong (and they always do), it's never their fault. They'll pin it on IT, Marketing, the intern, Mercury in retrograde — anyone but themselves. The only thing they manage consistently is accountability evasion.

The Resume Magician

Their LinkedIn reads like the biography of a Fortune 500 CEO. "Visionary Leader." "Strategic Innovator." "Global Change Agent." Translation: they once restarted the Wi-Fi router and remembered to reply-all on an email.

The Executive Whisperer

They might be useless to you, but to upper management? They're golden. Mystery Manager has perfected the art of sucking up. They laugh too hard at the CEO's jokes, always compliment the boss's tie, and somehow always get the best projects despite contributing nothing.

The Survivor's Smirk

Layoffs, mergers, restructures — they live through them all. Everyone else packs boxes. Mystery Manager just shrugs, finds a new title, and emerges unscathed. They're less an employee and more a corporate fungus: impossible to kill, always spreading.

Survival Guide

Speak Fluent Nonsense

If you want to survive, you need to learn their language: empty buzzwords. Stop saying, *"We should fix the process."* Start saying, *"We need to realign our operational synergies for maximum impact."* They won't know what it means — but they'll nod like you've just reinvented capitalism.

Perfect the Strategic Nod

In meetings, your best move isn't contributing — it's nodding. Nod at the right time, with the right amount of fake admiration. It convinces them they've made a "great point," buys you safety, and reduces the odds of them randomly derailing your project out of boredom.

Build Your Underground Network

You'll never get actual guidance from them, so you'll need allies. Befriend people in other departments, cling to competent managers, and trade information like you're running a black-market of sanity. Survival depends on knowing who actually knows things.

Document Everything

Mystery Manager loves to claim your ideas as their own. Keep email receipts, version histories, and timestamped files. That way, when the CEO says, *"Great idea, boss,"* you can at least whisper to your coworkers, *"Actually, that was mine."* Small victories count.

Play the Blame Game — Better

When projects implode, and they will, Mystery Manager will point fingers faster than a broken compass. Protect yourself by always having a scapegoat ready. Think of it as self-defense in the corporate Hunger Games.

Treat It Like Reality TV

At some point, the only way to keep your sanity is to stop pretending this is serious work. Pretend you're watching *The Office* unfold in real time. Grab popcorn. Place bets with your coworkers. *"Ten bucks says they misuse 'paradigm shift' before lunch."*

Keep Your Exit Strategy Warm

If all else fails, remember this: their incompetence is a gift. They're proof you don't want to spend your career here. So polish that résumé, build that LinkedIn profile, and keep your options open. Because when they finally tank the department, you'll be ready to bounce.

Bonus Activity: Mystery Manager Bingo

Play along during your next "strategy session" and see how long it takes to get a full row. Spoiler: not long.

Says "synergy" three times in one sentence
Forgets their own password in front of IT
Calls a 2-hour meeting with no agenda
Forwards your idea back to you as their own
Quotes Steve Jobs out of context
Claims they're "too high level" to send an email
Nods sagely at a buzzword they clearly don't understand
Uses a new acronym incorrectly
Laughs too hard at the CEO's joke
Brags about being "in back-to-back meetings all day"
Mispronounces a client's name — twice
Says "circle back" without circling back
Schedules a "strategy session" about staplers
Credits themselves for a win they weren't even present for
Blames another department within the first five minutes
Shares a meaningless "thought leadership" post on LinkedIn
Claims they're "working on a high-level initiative" nobody's heard of
Sends a recap email longer than the Bible
Smirks during layoffs but somehow keeps their job
Leaves early "for an executive offsite" (translation: golf)

Full house = permission to drink heavily.

Why Justice Never Comes

Here's the thing: everyone knows they're incompetent. The team knows. The clients know. Even the intern who's been here three weeks knows. And yet — somehow — Mystery Manager not only survives, they *thrive*. Promotions keep rolling in. Titles keep getting fancier. Their salary inflates like a helium balloon.

Why? Because the system is rigged for them.

The Confidence Con

They don't hesitate. They don't second-guess. They don't say, *"I'll get back to you."* They open their mouth, spray a handful of buzzwords into the air, and let confidence do the rest. In corporate life, confidence beats competence every time — and they've got confidence on tap.

The Executive Safety Blanket

Upper management loves them. Not because they're useful, but because they're predictable. Mystery Manager never rocks the boat. They never challenge authority. They nod, they smile, they laugh at every joke, and they always agree with the CEO's latest "vision." To the higher-ups, they're safe. And safe gets promoted.

The Blame Sponge

When things go wrong, they're experts at sliding blame downhill. IT didn't deliver. Marketing didn't execute. Finance didn't budget correctly. By the time anyone notices the truth — that they're the problem — the damage has already been buried under five layers of scapegoats.

The Illusion of Productivity

Mystery Manager is never idle. They're always *visible*. Not productive, but visible. They're in meetings, on calls, sending recap emails, cc'ing every living being in the company. It doesn't matter that the content is garbage — visibility is mistaken for value.

The Politics Play

Office politics is their Olympic sport. They network sideways, upwards, diagonally. They remember birthdays, flatter egos, and know exactly who to avoid pissing off. While you're working late to fix spreadsheets, they're at happy hour buying the VP a drink. Guess who gets noticed at promotion time?

The Beige Shield

Here's the genius: they're never *too bad*. They screw up constantly, but never catastrophically. They're just bland enough to avoid flames, just safe enough to keep around, and just shameless enough to claim wins that weren't theirs. Beige doesn't inspire firing squads. Beige just... lingers.

And that's why justice never comes. Because Mystery Manager isn't succeeding despite incompetence — they're succeeding *because* of it. They're the embodiment of corporate mediocrity: safe, confident, and indestructible.

Final Roast

The Over-Promoted Mystery Manager isn't a leader. They're a corporate hologram — projected into existence by buzzwords, nepotism, and sheer dumb luck. They don't manage people, projects, or outcomes. They manage to exist. That's it.

They are proof that meritocracy is a fairy tale. That effort, skill, and talent are optional, but confidence and networking are mandatory. They've built a career not on what they've done, but on what they've *made people think* they've done. And the wild part? It worked.

They are the human embodiment of beige wallpaper: boring, bland, impossible to remove, and somehow always getting a fresh coat of paint instead of being torn down. They've failed upward so many times they've hit orbit. While the rest of us scrape and claw for recognition, they simply float along, gathering promotions like lint.

And yes, it's infuriating. Watching them strut around the office, spouting nonsense, being praised for work you did, makes you want to flip your desk and walk out. But here's the sting: they'll outlast you. They'll still be here when you've quit, when the company rebrands, when the industry changes, when the building itself is condemned.

Because they're indestructible. Not because they're good — but because mediocrity, packaged correctly, is immortal.

So laugh. Laugh at the buzzwords, the incompetence, the endless parade of "strategy sessions" that achieve nothing. Laugh because while they may look like they're winning, they'll never be respected, never be admired, never be remembered as anything other than the punchline to the question: *"How the hell did they get here?"*

Because clowns can juggle, sure. But Mystery Manager? They're just holding the balls and pretending it's part of the act.

Chapter Fourteen
Conclusion: Welcome to the Circus

CONCLUSION: WELCOME TO THE CIRCUS

And there you have it — your very own field guide to the clowns, carnies, and chaos merchants who make office life feel less like work and more like a psychological endurance test.

You've met the **Idea Thief**, stealing brilliance like a raccoon in a dumpster. You've been cornered by the **Close Talker**, suffocating on secondhand coffee breath. You've survived **Calamity Jane**, who treats the office Christmas party like it's Fear Factor. You've smelled **Weird Smell Guy** before you've seen him. You've endured **Pill-Popping Penny**, who's practically a pharmaceutical start-up in heels. You've watched the **Career Olympian** sprint over your dignity on their way up the ladder. You've covered your eyes during **Vegas Vicki's** fashion crimes. You've lost years of your life to the **Meeting Hog.** You've marveled at the sheer audacity of the **Transient Supermodel.** You've endured the micromanaging breath on your neck, the smug smirk of **Half-Day Stella,** the email spam of **Pass-the-Buck Pete,** the hollow sighs of the **Retired-in-Spirit Guy,** and finally, the unkillable incompetence of the **Over-Promoted Mystery Manager.**

If reading this has given you flashbacks, congratulations: you've lived it. These people aren't just archetypes — they're real. They're sitting two desks away from you right now. They're proof that office life isn't built on logic or merit — it's built on endurance, caffeine, and the ability to laugh instead of cry.

Because that's the secret, isn't it? You can't escape them. HR won't save you. Promotions won't protect you. Transferring departments only swaps one set of clowns for another. The only real survival strategy is humor. To look at the madness around you, shrug, and say: *"Well, at least I'll get a good story out of this."*

So the next time you're cornered by a Close Talker, robbed by an Idea Thief, or watching Half-Day Stella waltz out at noon, remember: this is your cheap therapy. Laughter is the only HR-approved coping mechanism that won't end in paperwork.

And maybe, just maybe, one day you'll write your own chapter in this circus of incompetence. After all — clowns can juggle, sure. But in the office? They juggle us.

Also by Michelle Ward
Friends, Family and Other F*ck Ups
Because blood may be thicker than water, but it's also way messier. Survive your loud uncles, passive-aggressive aunts, drunk cousins, and friends who should've stayed home. Packed with cheap therapy laughs, awkward survival tips, and bingo cards to get you through even the most deranged holiday dinner.
Available now on Amazon.

Coming Soon in The Cheap Therapy Series
Exes and Other Emotional Support Disasters
Breakups, breakdowns, and the text you should've never sent.

Bosses and Other Broken PowerPoints
The mysteriously promoted, the terminally clueless, and the corporate cockroaches who will outlive us all.

Adulting and Other Modern Malfunctions
From bills and burnout to meal-prep shame and your neighbour's MLM invite — a survival manual for life itself.

All coming soon to Amazon, because therapy is expensive and sarcasm is free.

www.ingramcontent.com/pod-product-compliance
Lightning Source LLC
LaVergne TN
LVHW051602070426
835507LV00021B/2727